S0-BEZ-443

S·I·N·G·L·E M·A·L·T

Whisky

THE ILLUSTRATED IDENTIFIER TO 80 OF THE FINEST MALTS

S·I·N·G·L·E M·A·L·T

Whisky

THE ILLUSTRATED IDENTIFIER TO 80 OF THE FINEST MALTS

Helen Arthur

CHARTWELL
BOOKS, INC.

A QUINTET BOOK

Published by Chartwell Books
A Division of Book Sales, Inc.
114, Northfield Avenue
Edison, New Jersey 08837

This edition produced for sale in the U.S.A., its
territories and dependencies only.

Copyright© 1998 Quintet Publishing Limited.
All rights reserved. No part of this publication may be
reproduced, stored in a retrieval system or transmitted
in any form or by any means, electronic, mechanical,
photocopying, recording or otherwise, without the
permission of the copyright holder.

ISBN 0-7858-1027-7

This book was designed and produced by
Quintet Publishing Limited
6 Blundell Street
London N7 9BH

Creative Director: Richard Dewing
Designer: Steve West
Project Editors: Doreen Palamartschuk, Debbie Foy
Editor: Andrew Armitage

Typset in Great Britain by
Central Southern Typesetters, Eastbourne
Manufactured in Singapore by Eray Scan PTE LTD
Printed in Singapore by Star Standard Industries PTE LTD

The Publisher would like to thank all of the individual distilleries and their owning
companies for contributing illustrative material to support their entries in this book.
Additional picture credits go to the following:

Morrison Bowmore Distillers Ltd., pp.2, 11, 13, 31; Matthew Gloag & Son, p.7;
Allied Distillers Ltd., pp.8, 10, 15, 44; Burn Stewart Distillers PLC., p.12;
Life File Photographic Agency, pp.16, 19, 20, 26, 42, 47, 48, 53;
Whyte & Mackay Group, p.38; United Distillers, pp.34, 73.

While every effort has been made to ensure that all credits are listed,
the Publisher apologizes for any omissions.

CONTENTS

A SHORT HISTORY OF WHISKY

Before we look at the history of whisky, let us sort out a little puzzle. Is it whisky or whiskey? Generally, whisky is made in Scotland and whiskey is made in Ireland and the United States. Confusingly, however, most whiskies marketed in Japan and Canada are labeled "whisky." Malt whisky is the product of malted barley only. Grain whisky and whiskey from Ireland and the United States are produced from a wider range of cereals, including rye, wheat, and corn.

The first reference to making Scotch whisky dates from 1494, when Friar John Cor of Lindores Abbey, Fife, Scotland, is cited as purchasing eight bolts of malt, which would have produced 35 cases.

Home whisky distillation was permitted under the law and was a logical part of a Scottish farmer's economy. Following the English Civil War in 1643, the puritanical Government raised duty (taxes) on the importation of spirits from the Netherlands and alcoholic beverages that were produced at home. At first this did not affect Scotland, which was not then under English rule. However, the growth of whisky production prompted the Scottish Parliament to pass an Act in 1644 imposing an excise duty on spirits. Collecting taxes was very difficult as many distilleries were in remote and inaccessible places. In 1707, the Act of Union brought Scotland under English legislation, and laws were passed to control distillation. However, illegal distilling continued—and in many cases the illegal stills were designed so as to render them easy to take down and hide.

An 1823 Act of Parliament made distilling legal provided a license fee was paid, and the distillery produced more than 40 U.S. gallons a year. Then, in 1840, duty was imposed on each bottle sold by the distillery. This legalization of whisky production meant that permanent distilleries were built, the first to take out a license being The Glenlivet (1824), closely followed by Cardhu, The Glendronach, Old Fettercairn, and The Macallan—among others. The earliest recorded commercial whisky distilleries date back to the late eighteenth century and include Bowmore (1779), Highland Park (1798), Lagavulin (1784), and Tobermory (1795).

In 1863 an outbreak of phylloxera in France began to decimate the vineyards, and by 1879 most European vineyards had been forced to destroy their vines. Production of wine and, more importantly, cognac came to a halt and customers had to look elsewhere for their liquor. Attention turned to the homegrown product.

At this time Adrian Usher had been experimenting with whisky blending in Edinburgh and came up with a lighter, more palatable drink, more likely to appeal to the popular taste. Many new distilleries were built during this time, such as Benriach (1898), The Balvenie (1892), and Dufftown (1896).

Growth in whisky sales halted in 1898 when Pattison's, a well-known blending company, went bankrupt. Many distilleries closed through undercapitalization, overspending, and a general decline in the economic climate.

Marketing malt whisky became harder, as competition increased. It was not until 1963 that there was specific interest in single malts, however, as most were destined to satisfy the demand for blended whiskies. Several companies, notably William Grant & Sons, who placed considerable resources behind The Glenfiddich, started to market single malts aggressively.

High employment and marketing costs meant that many distilleries were unable to survive on their own. The growth of groups such as United Distillers ensured that many of these distilleries could continue producing whisky. Revival of interest in malt whisky in recent years has persuaded a few entrepreneurs to set up their own businesses, and a few distilleries are now in independent hands again.

Traditional whisky pagoda, Highland Park, Orkney

HOW WHISKY IS MADE

M alt whisky is the marriage of water, malted barley, and yeast. This apparently simple recipe belies the complexity of a drink made up of different colors, aromas, and tastes, which are produced by distilleries in various parts of Scotland.

A pure, clear water source is the starting point for making a good single malt whisky. And, as the water tumbles down from the Scottish hills or across peat bogs to the distillery, it will carry with it a little of its birthplace and travels—peat, heather, and granite. Whisky also needs heat from peat fires, the consummate skill of the distillery team, the magic of copper stills, maturation in oak casks, and good ventilation before it is considered ready for the market.

Many things make one malt different from that of a neighboring distillery: the water, type of barley, how long it is steeped in water, how long it is dried, whether peat is used in the drying process, and many more. Sometimes, more fanciful reasons are given such as the normally damp atmosphere in Scotland, the way the wind blows, or simply the magic of still and cask. Perhaps no one really knows the answer.

Traditional floor maltings – turning barley by hand

Malting barley

The production process starts with barley. All distilleries have their own sources of barley, and managers liaise closely with farmers to ensure that the raw material meets their requirements.

Barley is steeped in water for a couple of days and then allowed to germinate. In a traditional distillery the wet barley is spread out by hand on a concrete malting floor for about seven days. During this period the barley is turned frequently to ensure that the temperature is maintained at the required level and to control the rate of germination. At some distilleries the traditional wooden shovel—or shiel— *Adding water to the* is still used to turn the barley. Only a few remaining distilleries still malt their *mash tun* own barley, most purchasing it direct from maltings, where the grain is turned mechanically.

Once the required level of germination has been achieved, the natural enzymes in the barley are released. These produce soluble starch, which converts into sugar during the mashing process. Germination is arrested by drying the barley either over a peat fire or with warm air.

Distilleries throughout Scotland use some barley dried over peat fires. However, many Speyside and Lowland distilleries produce single malt whiskies that contain no peaty influences. The reason for the high peat content in some Islay whiskies can be explained by the fact that this was traditionally the only local source of local fuel, unlike in Campbeltown and Speyside, where coal was readily available. Peat fires in the different regions of Scotland produce a different range of tastes.

After a rest period, the dried malt is ground to a fine grist. This process is known as mashing. The grist—part flour, part solids—is placed in a container known as a mash tun and boiling water is added. Distillery managers jealously guard their water supplies, which help to give each malt whisky its particular flavor and aroma.

The shape and size of mash tuns vary, but they are normally of copper and usually have a lid. The boiling water dissolves the flour and releases the sugars in the barley. The resultant liquid, now known as wort, is drawn off from the base of the mash tun through the finely slotted bottom, cooled, and passed into fermentation vessels, or washbacks. The solids—draff, as they are known in Scotland—are removed from the mash tun and used as cattle feed.

Fermentation

Yeast is added either in liquid or solid form to the liquid wort, which has been cooled to around 70°C (158°F) in the large wooden washbacks. The yeast starts to ferment immediately and the mixture begins to give off carbon dioxide and foam. Scottish malt distillers use covered washbacks with lids that incorporate a rotating blade, which stops the foam pouring over the sides.

The sugars are converted into alcohol and, after about 48 hours, a warm, sweet, peaty beer with an alcoholic content of around 7.5% is achieved.

Distillation

The fermented wort, or wash, is then piped to the still room. Traditionally, stills in a Scottish malt whisky distillery are made of copper. All spirits stills are handmade and every distillery has stills of a different shape and size. The size and shape of the still and the skill of the stillman contribute to the quality of the final product. Only a small part of each distillate will go on to make malt whisky. Normally, malt whisky is produced after two distillations, but in some Lowland and Irish distilleries the spirit is distilled three times.

The spirit safe at The Glendronach

The first and largest still is the wash still, where the wash is boiled so that

it breaks down into its constituent parts and the alcohol can be drawn off. The boiling point of alcohol is lower than that of water, so it is the first vapor to rise up the neck of the still. The vapor produced is passed into a condenser—a series of pipe coils running through cold water. The angle of the pipe—or lyne arm—connecting the still to the condenser will affect the quality and speed of condensation.

From the condenser, the liquid, now called low wines, is collected in the spirit still for redistilling via the spirit safe. It is here that the involvement of the British Customs and Excise department begins. All spirits are subject to customs duty in the U.K. and production is strictly controlled to ensure that the correct amount is paid to Customs and Excise. Locks are fitted to the spirit safe by a Customs and Excise representative and measurements are taken of the spirit produced. The spirit safe contains several glass bowls into which the spirit can be directed using external faucets by the stillman. The low wines contain about 30% alcohol and must be distilled again in a spirit still, because they are unpalatable. Spirit stills are usually smaller than wash stills. The second distillation, which produces the pure spirit, is a carefully orchestrated and very precise procedure.

The stillman will start to test the spirit as soon as the rising vapors are condensed and pass through the spirit safe. He will direct the first liquid, which is known as foreshots, to the glass bowls in the spirit safe. These drain off into a collecting tank at the back of the stillroom. Foreshots turn cloudy when they come into contact with water, as they are still impure. The stillman can test the spirit in the spirit safe by adding water at regular intervals and checking the specific gravity.

Traditional copper spirit stills at Auchentoshan

As soon as the spirit starts to run clear, the stillman will immediately turn the faucets on the outside of the spirit safe and direct the spirit into what is known as the spirits receiver. To ensure the clarity and purity of the spirit, the speed of distillation is normally reduced at this stage. The stillman will continue to check the specific gravity and clarity of the spirit. After several hours, the spirit will start to weaken. This weakened spirit—or feints—is also discarded, and the stillman will then divert it to the low wines and feints-collecting tank.

In some distilleries, notably Bushmills in Northern Ireland and Auchentoshan in the Lowlands region, the spirit passes through a third still to produce a lighter whisky. This is known as triple distillation.

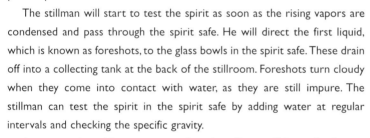

A watery residue remains in the still once the feints have been collected. This residue is called spent lees, and it is normally discharged into the sewer after treatment. Occasionally spent lees are sprayed over farmland.

The foreshots and feints will be added to the next wash for distillation, when the process will be repeated.

Maturation

The spirit is colorless, crude, and fiery—at this stage it has some of the characteristics of whisky but none of its final elegance. It now has to mature in barrels for three years before it can legally be called whisky. During this time the spirit will become softer and will start to turn color as the residues of bourbon, sherry, or port in the wood casks it is stored in are absorbed.

The spirit is stored in oak casks, which, according to their previous use, will have a bearing on the finished product

The immature spirit is piped into the filling room, where it is poured into oak barrels. Distillery managers exercise very stringent controls to ensure that the spirit is carefully measured as it is piped into barrels for maturation.

SPIRIT VAT
CONTENT 33050 Ltrs

All whisky warehouses are bonded: this means they hold goods in bond by the Government and every barrel is accounted for, so that the appropriate amount of duty is paid at the time of bottling.

Each distillery uses different types of barrels: some use only barrels in which American bourbon was once stored; others use sherry casks; some malt whiskies are finished in old port and old Madeira casks. Obviously, this helps to determine the final color and flavor of the malt whisky.

Once the barrels are filled, they are stored in bonded warehouses for a minimum of three years. If they are to be used for a single malt whisky or for a deluxe blend, the barrels will be stored for at least 10 to 15 years.

As wood is permeable, the surrounding air will seep into the whisky. If the air is salty, seaweedy, or heather-scented, for example, this adds to the characteristics of the malt. Some spirit will seep out, of course; many distillery managers quaintly describe this as "the angels' share." The temperature and humidity of the warehouses will also affect maturation. The longer a malt whisky is left to mature in the barrel, the more changes will take place, which is why malts of varying ages from the same distillery are so different.

From time to time, the barrels are tapped to check that all is well. A firm resonant sound means that the barrel is intact and the whisky is maturing well. A leaking or broken barrel produces a dull sound and the distillery manager knows that the barrel must be inspected and probably replaced.

The manager will draw a small amount from the barrel and pour it into a nosing glass. He—or she, but it tends to be a man's domain—will nose or smell the whisky and swirl it around in the glass, looking for a "string of pearls" around the surface of the liquid that shows him that the whisky is maturing satisfactorily. He will then return it to the barrel. (See pages 14–15 for how to taste the finished product.)

In the past, distillery workers were given old casks in which whisky had matured for many years. The casks were filled with hot water and steam and then rolled down the street. This produced several gallons of spirit. Unfortunately for today's distillery workers, this practice is no longer legal.

A whisky nosing glass. Its curvature and glass "lid" help to confine the aromas

Maturing slowly; whisky for the future

TASTING AND ENJOYING SINGLE MALT WHISKY

A single malt whisky is not just drunk, but savored. The following notes and advice will help you to learn more about whiskies and to understand the tasting notes in the Directory on pages 23–77.

First-time drinkers of single malt whiskies may not wish to invest in a full bottle right away. Whiskies are also available as miniatures, and this is a good way to start. Many restaurants and hotels throughout the world offer a good selection of single malt whiskies for the whisky drinker to taste and enjoy.

For newcomers to single malt whiskies, a drop of water should be added, ideally from the same source as the distillery uses, although this is mostly impracticable and bottled spring water is recommended. The addition of water reduces the intensity of flavor and allows the palate to savor the different tastes. Drinking a cask-strength malt whisky without adding water can be quite a shock to the system, and could put you off Scotch for life.

Start with the softer Lowland malts, graduate to Speyside, and then try malts from Orkney, Mull, Jura, and Islay. This way you will come to learn the differences in each malt and appreciate the distinct flavors of heather, peat, moorland, and sea.

Before you taste your whisky, look at the color. Every malt has its own particular color, from the palest gold to the darkest brown. This is the result of the maturation process, which takes place in plain oak, bourbon, sherry, port, or Madeira casks, imparting its colour and flavor to the whisky.

Pour a little into a glass, and cover the glass with your hand for a while to allow the aroma to gather. Move your hand away a little to uncover the scent. (The whisky blender uses a nosing glass similar to a sherry glass, which confines the vapors and makes it easier to identify the different aromas.)

Now take your hand away from the top of the glass and swirl the whisky around to release other fragrances. Sip the malt slowly. As you roll it around your tongue, distinct taste sensations will be experienced in different parts of the mouth.

Note how the taste changes as you swallow the whisky. This is known as the finish. Some single malt whiskies will have a more pronounced range of aftertastes than others.

Glassware

Part of the enjoyment of any spirit will come from the choice of glassware. A wide variety is available to the whisky drinker, and we have given some of the more popular types of glass below.

Crystal Traditionally, whisky is drunk from a small cut-glass tumbler. A cut-glass decanter filled with whisky, surrounded by several tumblers, can be very beautiful with refracted light changing the whisky from golden to ruby to amber. Edinburgh Crystal has been making such crystal for more than 125 years, but its origins can be traced back to the seventeenth century.

Plain glass Some whisky drinkers prefer plain glass so they can see the color more easily. Professional tasters use a nosing glass, which has a distinctive shape, and is supplied with a glass cover to allow the fragrances to gather inside the glass.

Centuries ago, the favorite drinking cup throughout Scotland was the quaich

Quaich This word is from the Gaelic *cuach*, meaning "shallow cup." This originated in the western Highlands, and certain sizes became reputed whisky measures. One of these was generally used when offering the cup of welcome to the visitor and serving the farewell cup. The primitive wood form was superseded by horn and then silver. Its simple shape with two handles or ears—known as "lugs"—remains unchanged.

WHISKY REGIONS

Here we will look mainly at the regions of Scotland, where most single malt whisky comes from, but we shall also look briefly at whisky regions elsewhere in the world—notably Japan and Northern Ireland.

Just as the wines of France are grouped according to their region of origin, so too are the malt whiskies of Scotland.

Lowlands

The Lowlands of Scotland with their undulating countryside do not immediately spring to mind as the home of Scotch whisky, which mostly conjures up images of mountains and tumbling streams. However, whisky needs a ready supply of fine barley and pure water, and this region has both. Most Lowland malts are produced with very little peat. The notable exception is Glenkinchie, which is a slightly dry, smoky malt.

Historically, the Lowland region, situated below an imaginary line linking the Clyde and Tay rivers, produced whisky in large industrial stills, which had none of the delicacy or range of flavors of the Highland malts. However, these are all long gone and the few remaining distilleries produce fine malts which are characteristically lighter, without the taste of peat or the sea.

Lowland malts are not affected by the strong winds off the sea, as island malts are, and there is little salt in the finished product.

Highlands

As the traveler takes the road north from the Speyside region there are fewer distilleries. The road takes you past the site of the now dismantled Glen Albyn Distillery and to the distilleries of Glen Ord, Teaninch, Dalmore, Glenmorangie, Balblair, and Clynelish, and then, at the end of the road, near Wick, is Pulteney, the northernmost distillery on the mainland of Scotland. These distilleries are referred to as being in the Northern Highlands, a

mountainous part of Scotland where streams tumbling over granite, heather hills, and glens introduce interesting flavors and aromas to the whiskies.

In this region each whisky is different from its neighbor and owes its characteristics to the local topography and water supply. This is a spectacularly beautiful part of Scotland, with some very rewarding views. The malts produced on Mull, Jura, and Orkney are also included in this region.

The Orkney Isles

At the northern tip of Scotland lie the Orkneys, a group of islands with the Atlantic to the west and the North Sea to the east. The Orkneys are fertile with rolling countryside.

The islands' natural resources—a plentiful supply of water, fertile soil for growing barley, and a large supply of peat—historically meant that whisky distillation could carry on undisturbed.

Orkney whiskies smell of sea air, which seeps into the wooden barrels as it matures in warehouses close to the sea. Peat on the island, which is used to dry the malted barley, is made from heather, and this imparts a honey to the whisky.

Speyside

The Speyside whisky region sits in the Highlands of Scotland. The River Spey flows between the Ladder and Cromdale Hills into the Grampian Hills. This mountainous region was virtually inaccessible during the seventeenth and early eighteenth centuries, and so illegal distilling was a favorite pastime.

Many distilleries in this area use underground springs for their water supply, and the purity of the water contributes to the final product. The individual distilleries in Speyside produce different malts, but most of them have a characteristic balance of sweetness, for Speyside malts are made using very little peat.

Campbeltown

A century ago a visitor to Campbeltown would probably have arrived by boat. As the town and surrounding area came into view nearly 30 distillery chimneys would have been silhouetted against the skyline. For this was once the heart of whisky-making, but now, sadly, the number of distilleries is reduced to two—Springbank and Glen Scotia.

The sea air of the Mull of Kintyre, on which Campbeltown is situated, imparts a special flavor to these malts.

Islay

The island of Islay is on the west coast of Scotland off the Mull of Kintyre, and is the most fertile of the Hebridean Islands, which run along the west coast of Scotland.

Islay is a beautiful, windswept island with rugged hills, deep wooded valleys, miles of open moorland, and rolling agricultural countryside. The seven distilleries on the island produce very different malt whiskies, from the light Bunnahabhain and Caol Ila to the stronger, aromatic Laphroaig and Ardbeg.

Northern Ireland

There are many links between Northern Ireland and Scotland. They share a common language—Gaelic, which has since developed differently for each country—and the landscape is similar, with its large lakes, tumbling streams, peat bogs, rolling agricultural countryside, and mountains. Indeed, legend would have it that the Giant's Causeway, off the coast of County Antrim, was a footpath to Scotland.

Bushmills is the oldest recorded distillery and is situated at Coleraine in County Antrim on a line to the south of the Mull of Kintyre and thus, further south than most distilleries in Scotland.

Eire

The art of distilling whiskey was well known in Ireland by the fourteenth century. Much of the current production is distilled using a mixture of grains and unmalted barley, oats, wheat, and rye. Several distilleries produce single malts. Eire is south of Scotland and the more temperate climate produces whiskeys with a slightly spicier taste and a crisp finish.

Japan

Japanese whisky owes its origins to Scotland. The first distillers were trained there, and took their new-found knowledge to traditional sake distilleries in Japan. The landscape of the northern island, Hokkaido, is very similar to that of the Highlands of Scotland, with peat bogs, mountains, and cool, fresh streams, which flow over granite rocks, but the peat produces a less intense aroma than Scottish peat.

Tasmania

Andrew Morrison, a farmer in Tasmania, has started to produce a single malt whisky at Cradle Mountain Distillery. Tasmania has an ideal climate for producing whisky, and the right local ingredients.

THE DIRECTORY
OF WHISKY

This directory lists distilleries whose single malt whiskies are available worldwide. Most of the whisky distilleries are fully operational, but some have been closed down for a while and could reopen at any time. The industry uses the term "mothballed" when distilleries are temporarily closed.

Whiskies are included here mainly from Scotland, of course, but also from Northern Ireland and Japan. Unfortunately, not all whiskies were available for tasting. In Japan, there are at least a dozen malt whisky distilleries, but most of their production is sold at home and very little is exported.

In Eire, at the Cooley Distillery, two single malts are produced—Tyrconnell and Connemara—and in Tasmania Cradle Mountain single malt whisky is now available.

The whiskies are in alphabetical order and listings show which country they come from and, in the case of Scotland, the region in which each distillery is located. Each region is color-coded for easy reference.

The introduction on each page gives the key information about the distillery, along with when it was founded, often by whom, its phone and fax numbers, and visiting information where appropriate.

You will see a number of symbols under the heading DISTILLERY FACTS on each entry. These tell you when the distillery was founded, its water source, the number and types of stills it uses (wash still, spirit still, for instance; see How Whisky is Made, beginning on page 8), what sort of casks are used for maturing, and some visiting information. Specific visiting times have not been included because they could change, and you are advised to phone the distillery for times and seasons. Current owners of distilleries have not been included because of the often fast-changing nature of the food-and-drink industry, which is frequently the subject of takeovers and mergers. Any information that was not available at the time of writing has been marked N/A.

KEY TO THE DIRECTORY

Each brand is accompanied by tasting notes. The information here covers age, nose, and taste, all based on the author's personal opinion. The symbols in the DISTILLERY FACTS sections are:

 Region

 Stills

 Founded

 Casks

 Water supply

 Visiting information

The color codes for each whisky region are featured below and are repeated in the directory section for ease of reference.

Lowlands	
Highlands	
Speyside	
Islay	
Campbeltown	
Northern Ireland	
Japan	

ABERFELDY

ABERFELDY DISTILLERY, ABERFELDY, PERTHSHIRE PH15 2EB
TEL: +44 (0) 1887 820330 FAX: +44 (0) 1887 820432

Aberfeldy Distillery was founded in 1896 by John Dewar & Sons Ltd. and was built on the south bank of the River Tay. Long associated with whisky distilling, Aberfeldy's main water source is the Pitilie Burn, a brook that also supplied another distillery until 1867.

The distillery closed during World War II until 1945. In 1972–73 the distillery was rebuilt and outfitted with four new steam-heated stills.

DISTILLERY FACTS

	Highland		N/A
	1896		Easter–Oct. Phone
	Pitilie Burn		for times.
	2 wash 2 spirit		

TASTING NOTES

AGE: 15 years, 43%

NOSE: Warm; sherry and nutmeg

TASTE: Medium-bodied with a hint of smoke.

ABERLOUR

ABERLOUR DISTILLERY, ABERLOUR, BANFFSHIRE AB38 9PJ
TEL: +44 (0) 1340 871204 FAX: +44 (0) 1340 871729

The word *Aberlour* is Gaelic and means "Mouth of the Chattering Burn" and may have a connection with the well in the distillery grounds, dating back to when the valley was occupied by Druids. James Fleming founded the distillery in 1879, and it changed hands several times until S. Campbell & Sons Ltd. purchased it in 1945. Aberlour is a beautiful amber single malt.

DISTILLERY FACTS

	Speyside		2 wash 2 spirit
	1826		N/A
	Springs on Ben Rinnes		No visitors

TASTING NOTES

AGE: 10 years, 40%

NOSE: Heady malt and caramel aroma

TASTE: Medium-bodied with hints of peat and honey.

AN CNOC

KNOCKDHU DISTILLERY, KNOCK, BY HUNTLY, ABERDEENSHIRE AB5 5LJ
TEL: +44 (0) 1466 771223 FAX: +44 (0) 1466 771359

Knockdhu Distillery was built in 1893 for Haig's, when springs containing pure, crystal-clear water were discovered. This, together with good local supplies of barley and peat, provided the ideal raw materials. Production began in October 1894 and as many as 3,000 U.S. gallons were distilled each week. The distillery was bought by Inver House Distillers in 1988 and relaunched, using the name An Cnoc.

DISTILLERY FACTS

〰	Speyside	🅰	1 wash 1 spirit
🍐	1893	🛢	Oak hogsheads
〰	Springs at the foot of Knockdhu	ℹ	No visitors

TASTING NOTES

AGE: 12 years, 40%

NOSE: Soft aromatic, hint of vanilla ice cream and smoke

TASTE: Clean malt with full range of fruit flavors and a long, smooth finish. A malt for every occasion.

ARDBEG

ARDBEG DISTILLERY, PORT ELLEN, ISLE OF ISLAY PA42 7EB
TEL: +44 (0) 1496 302224

Distilling at Ardbeg began around 1798, but it was not until 1815 that the MacDougall family began commercial distilling. By 1886 Ardbeg was employing 60 people out of a population in the village of 200 and was producing 300,000 U.S. gallons of pure alcohol a year.

Ardbeg Distillery is now fully operational again and we look forward to tasting new stocks of this fine malt whisky in 10 or so years time.

DISTILLERY FACTS

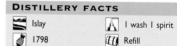

〰	Islay	🅰	1 wash 1 spirit
🍐	1798	🛢	Refill
〰	Loch Arinambeast and Uigedale	ℹ	No visitors

TASTING NOTES

AGE: 1974, 40%

NOSE: Full peaty aroma, slightly medicinal

TASTE: Smoky, rich, with an excellent rounded finish.

ARDMORE

ARDMORE DISTILLERY, KENNETHMONT, HUNTLY, ABERDEENSHIRE AB54 4NH
TEL: +44 (0) 1464 831213 FAX: +44 (0) 1464 831428

Ardmore Distillery was built by William Teacher & Sons in 1898. It is near the River Bogie, which is at the edge of the Grampians, the range of low mountains across central Scotland separating the Lowlands from the Highlands.

In 1955 the number of stills was increased from two to four, and in 1974 to eight. Many of the original distillery features are preserved on site, including coal-fired stills and a steam engine.

DISTILLERY FACTS

	Speyside		4 wash 4 spirit
	1898		N/A
	Local springs		No visitors

TASTING NOTES

AGE: 1981, 40%

NOSE: Sweet with promise

TASTE: Strong, malty, yet sweet on the palate with a dry finish. A good after-dinner malt.

AUCHENTOSHAN

AUCHENTOSHAN DISTILLERY, DALMUIR, DUNBARTONSHIRE G81 4SG
TEL: +44 (0) 1389 878561 FAX: +44 (0) 1389 877368

Auchentoshan was built in 1800 and passed through many hands until 1969 when it was sold to Eadie Cairns, who re-equipped the distillery. In 1984 it was purchased by Morrison-Bowmore Distilleries, owners—at the time of writing—of Glen Garioch and Bowmore Distilleries. The whisky is triple-distilled. It has a fresh, slightly lemony aroma with a warm color, reminiscent of sunny wheatfields.

DISTILLERY FACTS

	Lowland		Ex-bourbon and
	1800		sherry
	Loch Cochno		No visitors
	1 wash		
	1 intermediate spirit		

TASTING NOTES

AGE: Unaged, 40%

NOSE: Warm, slightly citrusy. Inviting

TASTE: Very smooth fruit flavors with a definite aftertaste.

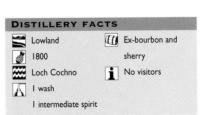

AULTMORE

Aultmore Distillery was founded in 1895 by Alexander Edward. It sits on Auchinderran Burn—*Aultmore* is Gaelic for "Big Burn." In 1898, Edward purchased the distillery at Oban and launched the Oban & Aultmore-Glenlivet Distilleries. Production at both distilleries was reduced in 1899 when Pattison's, the blenders, went into liquidation (see A Short History of Whisky on pp. 6–7). John Dewar & Sons bought Aultmore in 1923. It was one of the first distilleries to treat waste so it could be used for animal feed.

DISTILLERY FACTS

	Speyside		2 wash 2 spirit
	1895		N/A
	Auchinderran Burn		No visitors

TASTING NOTES

AGE: 12 years, 43%

NOSE: Delicate, summery, with a hint of honey and smoke

TASTE: Well-rounded malt with a warm, smooth, slightly buttery taste.

THE BALVENIE

THE BALVENIE DISTILLERY, DUFFTOWN, KEITH, BANFFSHIRE AB55 4DH
TEL: +44 (0) 1340 820373 FAX +44 (0) 1340 820805

The Balvenie Distillery occupies a site near the ancient Balvenie Castle and was built alongside the Glenfiddich Distillery by William Grant in 1892. Balvenie remains one of the most traditional distilleries in Scotland, using, wherever possible, barley grown nearby and its own floor maltings.

It produces very distinctive malts, two of which are the Balvenie Founders Reserve (10 years old) and the Balvenie Double Wood (12 years old). There is

DISTILLERY FACTS

	Speyside		Oak—Spanish
	1892		sherry and
	The Robbie Dubh		American bourbon
	Springs		No visitors
	4 wash 4 spirit		

TASTING NOTES

AGE: 10 years Founders Reserve, 40%

NOSE: Smoky with citrus and a hint of honey

TASTE: Dry, refreshing, with a rounded taste and a touch of sweetness.

AGE: 12 years Double Wood, 40%

NOSE: Glorious, rich

TASTE: Full-bodied, smooth on the palate with a fuller, sweeter finish.

also a limited edition of about 300 bottles of the Balvenie Single Barrel.

The Balvenie single malts vary in color from pale straw through golden honey to a rich deep amber with a hint of copper.

BEN NEVIS

BEN NEVIS, LOCH BRIDGE, FORT WILLIAM PM33 6TJ
TEL: +44 (0) 1397 702476 FAX: +44 (0) 1397 702768

Ben Nevis Distillery was built in 1825 by John Macdonald, known as Long John. Ben Nevis continued to grow and, in 1894, the West Highland Railway was officially opened, providing a cheap means of transporting coal to the distillery. It was sold in 1955 to Joseph Hobbs, who installed a Coffey still, but it was removed some years ago. Ben Nevis was purchased by the Nikka Whisky Distilling Company of Japan in 1989.

DISTILLERY FACTS

	Highland		Mix of fresh sherry
	1825		and bourbon, refill
	Alt a Mhulin on		sherry and
	Ben Nevis		hogsheads
	2 wash 2 spirit		Jan–Oct.

TASTING NOTES

AGE: 1970 26 years old, Cask No. 4533, 52.5%

NOSE: Fragrant with a sweet, full, aroma

TASTE: Full-bodied, very flavorful—sherry, caramel, peat—with a long, sweet finish.

BENRIACH

BENRIACH DISTILLERY, LONGMORN, NEAR ELGIN, MORAYSHIRE
TEL: +44 (0) 1542 783400 FAX: +44 (0) 1542 783404

Benriach was founded in 1898 by John Duff, whose other distillery at Longmorn was linked to Benriach by a railroad. The Benriach produced whisky for only two years before it closed in 1900, but the Longmorn Distilleries Co. Ltd. reopened the Benriach in 1965 and in 1978 it was purchased by Seagram Distillers Plc. In 1994 Benriach was released for the first time as a 10-year-old single malt.

DISTILLERY FACTS

	Speyside		N/A
	1898		By appointment
	Local Springs		only
	2 wash 2 spirit		

TASTING NOTES

AGE: 10 years, 43%

NOSE: Elegant, delicate aroma with hint of summer flowers

TASTE: Light, soft with sweet fruit flavors, a dry aftertaste with a hint of peat.

BENRINNES

BENRINNES DISTILLERY, ABERLOUR, BANFFSHIRE AB38 9NN
TEL: +44 (0) 1340 871215 FAX: +44 (0) 1340 871840

Distilling was started here in 1826 by Peter McKenzie, although the current distillery was founded in 1835. The distillery was originally named Lyne of Ruthrie by John Innes, who, forced into bankruptcy, sold the farm and out-buildings for distilling to William Smith, who changed the name to Benrinnes. He too sold out and David Edward took over the distillery. In 1922 it was purchased by John Dewar & Sons.

DISTILLERY FACTS

	Speyside		2 wash 2 spirit
	1835		N/A
	Scurran and Rowantree Burns		No visitors

TASTING NOTES

AGE: Benrinnes 21 years, 1974, 60.4%

NOSE: Rich butterscotch

TASTE: Full-bodied, hint of vanilla and fruit, slightly oily texture and a warm lingering finish.

BENROMACH

BENROMACH DISTILLERY, FORRES, MORAYSHIRE IV35 0EB
TEL: +44 (0) 1343 545111 FAX: +44 (0) 1343 540155

Benromach Distillery was built in 1898 by Duncan McCallum of Glen Nevis Distillery and F.W. Brickman, a Leith spirit dealer. It closed almost immediately, but reopened in 1907 as Forres, with McCallum still at the helm. Revived as Benromach after World War I, the distillery was purchased by Associated Scottish Distillers in 1938, closed in 1983 by United Distillers, and purchased by Gordon & MacPhail in 1992.

DISTILLERY FACTS

	Speyside		N/A
	1898		No visitors
	Chapelton Springs		
	1 wash 1 spirit		

TASTING NOTES

AGE: 12 years, 40%

NOSE: Light, sweet, and fresh

TASTE: A good, rounded malt, light caramel with spice and a long, slightly strong finish.

BLAIR ATHOL

Founded in 1798 by John Stewart and Robert Robertson, Blair Athol Distillery passed through several hands until it was inherited by Elizabeth Conacher in 1860. It was then bought by a Liverpool wine merchant, Peter Mackenzie, who was born in Glenlivet—which gives its name to another famous malt. It closed in 1932, and was acquired by Arthur Bell & Sons, but did not reopen until 1949. The number of stills was increased from two to four in 1973.

The label on a bottle of Blair Athol depicts an otter. The distillery's water supply is the Allt Dour Burn which means

DISTILLERY FACTS		
Highland		Easter–Sep. and
1798		Oct.–Easter. Some
Allt Dour Burn		tours by
2 wash 2 spirit		appointment only;
N/A		please phone

TASTING NOTES

AGE: 12 years, 43%

NOSE: A cold hot toddy—fresh, honey and lemon

TASTE: Warm malt with a hint of sweetness and smoke.

"The Burn of the Otter." Blair Athol is a warm amber single malt whisky.

BOWMORE

BOWMORE DISTILLERY, BOWMORE, ISLAY, ARGYLL **PA43 7JS**
TEL: +44 (0) 1496 810441 FAX: +44 (0) 1496 810757

According to legend, the sea is red at Bowmore because, when the giant Ennis (Angus) was crossing Loch Indaal his dogs were killed by a dragon who had been woken from his slumbers. Like all Islay distilleries, Bowmore is built close to the seashore. At Bowmore, however, a warehouse is built below sea level and the Atlantic waves break against the thick walls, imparting a special flavor to the whisky in the barrels.

Bowmore, which produces a wide range of truly distinctive malts from its in-house maltings, was built in 1779 and is one of the earliest recorded distilleries in Scotland.

DISTILLERY FACTS

	Islay	ℹ	Weekdays.
	1779		Entrance fee
	River Laggan		redeemable in the
	2 wash 2 spirit		distillery shop
	Ex-bourbon and		
	sherry		

TASTING NOTES

AGE: Legend, 40%

NOSE: Peat with tang of the sea

TASTE: Flavors of sea and smoke with citrus and a fresh warming finish.

AGE: 12 years, 43%

NOSE: Light, smoky, stronger hint of the sea

TASTE: Round and satisfying with a long finish.

AGE: 17 years, 43%

NOSE: The smoky aroma has taken on hints of ripe fruits and flowers

TASTE: Honey, seaweed, toffee, and citrus with a long, mellow finish. Perfect after-dinner malt.

BRUICHLADDICH

BRUICHLADDICH, ISLAY, ARGYLL **PA49 7UN**
TEL: **+44 (0) 1496 850221**

Bruichladdich is Scotland's westernmost distillery and was built in 1881 by Robert, William, and John Gourlay. In 1886, the company was relaunched as Bruichladdich Distillery Co. (Islay) Ltd. and continued producing whisky until 1929, when it was silent for about eight years. It became part of Whyte & Mackay's whisky portfolio but at the time of writing is silent again, having been mothballed in 1995.

DISTILLERY FACTS

Islay		American white	
1881		oak	
Private reservoir		No visitors	
2 wash 2 spirit			

TASTING NOTES

AGE: 10 years, 40%

NOSE: A refreshing, subtle aroma

TASTE: Medium-bodied with a lingering flavor, undertones of citrus and peat— a light Islay malt.

BUNNAHABHAIN

BUNNAHABHAIN DISTILLERY, PORT ASKAIG, ISLE OF ISLAY, ARGYLL **PA46 7RR**
TEL: **+44 (0) 1496 840646** FAX: **+44 (0) 1496 840248**

Bunnahabhain Distillery was built in 1883 on a site chosen because of its accessibility by boat from the mainland and a ready supply of fresh peaty water. Initially, sales were made solely to the wholesale market for blended whisky. In the late 1970s, the owners, Highland Distilleries, launched a 12-year-old Bunnahabhain, a lightly peated malt with a soft, mellow character and a beautiful golden corn color.

DISTILLERY FACTS

Islay		Mix of bourbon	
1883		and sherry	
River Margadale		By appointment	
2 wash 2 spirit		only	

TASTING NOTES

AGE: 12 years, 40%

NOSE: Definite aroma of sea and summer flowers

TASTE: Just a hint of peat, light and malty. A richer, stronger finish. A favorite after-dinner drink.

BUSHMILLS

OLD BUSHMILLS, BUSHMILLS, CO. ANTRIM BT57 8XH
TEL: +44 (0) 1265 731521 FAX: +44 (0) 1265 731339

Bushmills is the oldest recorded licensed distillery in the U.K. The distillery was founded in 1608 and is situated not far from the site of the Giant's Causeway. Until 1988 Bushmills was owned by Irish Distillers, when it was acquired by Group Pernod-Ricard. Here, as at Auchentoshan, the whiskey (note the spelling of the Irish variety) is triple-distilled. This is a very distinctive whiskey with a full flavor, and is a firm favorite.

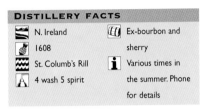

DISTILLERY FACTS

N. Ireland		Ex-bourbon and
1608		sherry
St. Columb's Rill	i	Various times in
4 wash 5 spirit		the summer. Phone
		for details

TASTING NOTES

AGE: 10 years, 40%

NOSE: Warm, honey with sherry and spice

TASTE: A warm, smooth malt with full flavors of sweetness and spice.

CAOL ILA

CAOL ILA DISTILLERY, PORT ASKAIG, ISLAY, ARGYLL PA46 7RL
TEL: +44 (0) 1496 840207 FAX: +44 (0) 1496 840660

The distillery was built in 1846 by Hector Henderson. In 1927 Distillers Co. Ltd. obtained a controlling interest in Caol Ila. The distillery was largely rebuilt in 1974 and the number of stills increased from two to six. Caol Ila is pale straw in colour and has a well-rounded, slightly peaty taste. This is a very good introduction to Islay malts.

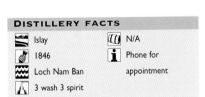

DISTILLERY FACTS

Islay		N/A
1846	i	Phone for
Loch Nam Ban		appointment
3 wash 3 spirit		

TASTING NOTES

AGE: 15 years, 43%

NOSE: Clean with the aromas of sea, smoke, and apples

TASTE: Mellow with a hint of the sea.

CARDHU

CARDHU DISTILLERY, KNOCKANDO, ABERLOUR, BANFFSHIRE AB38 7RY
TEL: +44 (0) 1340 810204 FAX: +44 (0) 1340 872554

Whisky was distilled illegally here until 1824, when John Cumming took out a license. Before that, he had relied on the isolated location of the farm to keep the excisemen at bay. However, excisemen would frequently stay at the farm, so Cumming's wife Ellen would raise a red flag once they were safely eating dinner, to warn other local distillers. Eventually, a new distillery was erected on land next to the farm buildings. Cardow, as it was then called, was purchased by John Walker & Sons Ltd. in 1893 and in 1925 the company merged with the Distillers Company Ltd. The distillery was rebuilt in 1960–61 and the number of stills increased from four to six. It changed its name from Cardow to Cardhu in 1981.

DISTILLERY FACTS

🏔	Speyside	🅰	3 wash 3 spirit
🌾	1824	🛢	N/A
〰	Springs on the Mannoch Hill and Lyne Burn	ℹ	Jan.–Dec., and May–Sep. Exhibition and picnic area

TASTING NOTES

AGE: 12 years, 40%

NOSE: Warm honey and spice—a hint of winter sunshine

TASTE: Fresh on the palate, hint of honey and nutmeg. Smooth finish.

CLYNELISH

CLYNELISH, BRORA, SUTHERLAND KW9 6LB
TEL: +44 (0) 1408 621444 FAX: +44 (0) 1408 623004

This distillery was founded in 1819 by the Marquess of Stafford, and was first licensed to James Harper. The lease changed hands several times until, in 1912, 50 percent of Clynelish was acquired by The Distillers Company Ltd. A new distillery was built nearby in 1967–68 and given the name Clynelish. The old distillery was closed, and reopened in April 1975 with the name Brora. Brora and Clynelish have the same water source, the Clynemilton Burn.

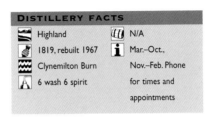

DISTILLERY FACTS

	Highland		N/A
	1819, rebuilt 1967		Mar.–Oct.,
	Clynemilton Burn		Nov.–Feb. Phone
	6 wash 6 spirit		for times and
			appointments

TASTING NOTES

AGE: Clynelish 23 years, distilled 1972, 57.1%

NOSE: Full of fruit and spice, warm, inviting

TASTE: Smooth, slightly dry at first, growing with fruit and sweetness, and a strong, flavorful finish.

CRAGGANMORE

CRAGGANMORE DISTILLERY, BALLINDALLOCH, BANFFSHIRE AB37 9AB
TEL: +44 (0) 1807 500202 FAX: +44 (0) 1807 500288

John Smith founded this distillery in 1869. He died in 1886 and Cragganmore continued under the management of his brother, George, then going to John's son, Gordon. In 1923 Gordon's widow sold the distillery to a group of businessmen. Cragganmore closed from 1941 to 1946. In 1964 it was extended, and the number of stills increased from two to four. Cragganmore became a member of the Distillers Co. in 1965.

DISTILLERY FACTS

	Speyside		N/A
	1869		Trade visitors only,
	Craggan Burn		by appointment
	2 wash 2 spirit		

TASTING NOTES

AGE: 12 years, 40%

NOSE: Dry, honey aroma

TASTE: A pleasant, medium-bodied malt with a short smoky finish.

CRAIGELLACHIE

CRAIGELLACHIE DISTILLERY, CRAIGELLACHIE, ABERLOUR, BANFFSHIRE AB38 9ST
TEL: +44 (0) 1340 881212 FAX: +44 (0) 1340 881311

Craigellachie Distillery was built by Alexander Edward in 1891. The distillery sits on a hillside above the village of Craigellachie. It was purchased in 1916 by Sir Peter Mackie, the father of White Horse Blended Whisky.

In 1927 Craigellachie was purchased by Distillers Co. The distillery was rebuilt in 1964 and the number of stills was increased from two to four.

DISTILLERY FACTS

〰	Speyside	⚏	2 wash 2 spirit
🌾	1891	⬡	N/A
〰	Little Conval Hill	ℹ	No visitors

TASTING NOTES

AGE: 22 years, 60.2%

NOSE: Strong, fully peaty aroma

TASTE: Deceptively light, medium-bodied, smoky and spicy.

DAILUAINE

DAILUAINE DISTILLERY, CARRON, ABERLOUR, BANFFSHIRE AB38 7RE
TEL: +44 (0) 1340 810361 FAX: +44 (0) 1340 810510

The distillery was founded by William Mackenzie in 1851 and its name means "green vale" in Gaelic. After Mackenzie's death, James Fleming of Aberlour took on the lease, and Mackenzie's son Thomas became a partner. Its name changed several times before his death in 1915. The company was then acquired by the Distillers Co. Much of the distillery was destroyed by fire in 1917, rebuilt soon after, and again in 1959–60.

DISTILLERY FACTS

🌊	Speyside	🅰	3 wash 3 spirit
🏭	1851	🛢	N/A
〰	Ballieumullich Burn	ℹ	No visitors

TASTING NOTES

AGE: Dailuaine 22 years, distilled 1973, 60.92%

NOSE: A full smoky aroma with a hint of honey

TASTE: Spicy, Christmas pudding on the tongue, with a long sweet finish.

DALLAS DHU

DALLAS DHU DISTILLERY, FORRES, MORAYSHIRE IV37 0RR
TEL: +44 (0) 1309 676548

Dallas Dhu was built in 1898 by Wright & Greig, whisky blenders in Glasgow, in association with Alexander Edward. In 1919 the company was purchased by J.R. O'Brien & Co., distillers in Glasgow, and ownership changed again in 1921 when the company was acquired by Benmore Distilleries of Glasgow. Dallas Dhu was bought by the Distillers Co. in 1929. It was closed by United Distillers in 1983 and is run as a living museum.

DISTILLERY FACTS

🌊	Speyside	🛢	N/A
🏭	1898	ℹ	Apr.–Sep., Oct.–Mar.
〰	Altyre Burn		Phone for details
🅰	N/A		

TASTING NOTES

AGE: 12 years, 40%

NOSE: Warm with sherry and peat

TASTE: A well-rounded malt with smoke and a warm, slightly oak finish.

THE DALMORE

DALMORE DISTILLERY, ALNESS, ROSS-SHIRE IV17 0UT
TEL: +44 (0) 1349 882362 FAX: +44 (0) 1349 883655

Dalmore means "big meadowland" and takes its name from the vast grassland of the Black Isle, which lies opposite the distillery in the Firth of Cromarty. The distillery was built in 1839 by Alexander Matheson, and was bought by the Mackenzie family in 1886. In 1960 they joined forces with Whyte & Mackay Ltd. to form Dalmore-Whyte & Mackay Ltd.

Production ceased during World War I. Saladin maltings were built there in 1956 and the number of stills doubled to eight in 1966. The flavor of Dalmore malt is influenced by the water, peated barley and sea winds.

DISTILLERY FACTS

	Highland		Mix of oloroso
	1839		sherry & American
	River Alness		white oak
	4 wash 4 spirit		Early Sep.–mid-June. Phone for appointment

TASTING NOTES

AGE: 12 years, 40%

NOSE: A fully, fruity aroma with hints of sherry sweetness

TASTE: A good, full-bodied malt with overtones of honey and spice with a dry finish.

DALWHINNIE

DALWHINNIE DISTILLERY, DALWHINNIE, INVERNESS-SHIRE PH19 1AB
TEL: +44 (0) 1528 522240

Dalwhinnie single malt is part of United Distillers' "Classic Malt" range. The distillery began operations as the Strathspey Distillery in 1898 and stands at a popular meeting place for drovers from the north and west. (*Dalwhinnie* means "meeting place" in Gaelic.)

The distillery's first owners were not successful and the distillery was soon purchased by A.P. Blyth. In 1905 it was sold to Cook & Bernheimer of New York for $2,000. It was acquired by Sir James Calder in 1920 and then, in 1926, by the Distillers Co. It closed after a fire in 1934, and did not reopen until after World War II.

DISTILLERY FACTS

Highland		N/A	
1898		Easter–Oct. Call	
Allt an t-Sluie Burn		+44 (0) 1528	
1 wash 1 spirit		522268 for	
		appointment	

TASTING NOTES

AGE: 15 years, 43%

NOSE: Dry, aromatic, summery

TASTE: A beautiful malt with hints of honey and a lush, sweet finish.

DEANSTON

DEANSTON DISTILLERY, DEANSTON, NEAR DOUNE, PERTHSHIRE FK16 6AG
TEL: +44 (0) 1786 841422 FAX: +44 (0) 1786 841439

Deanston Distillery is unique in that it is housed inside a historic building, an old cotton mill which was designed by the inventor Richard Arkwright. Cotton mills and whisky distilleries have a common requirement—a pure source of water. It stands on the banks of the River Teith, a river renowned for its salmon and the purity of its water. Both the main distillery building and maturation warehouses date from 1785. The building was converted into a working distillery in 1966 and was purchased by Burn Stewart in 1990.

Deanston is a pale gold malt with a smooth, mellow character. The 12-year-old includes a history of the Scottish Wars of Independence. Only 2,000 of the Deanston 25-year-old are produced each year.

DISTILLERY FACTS

Highland		2 wash 2 spirit	
1966		Refill and sherry	
River Teith		No visitors	

TASTING NOTES

AGE: 12 years, 40%

NOSE: A truly cereal aroma

TASTE: A malt flavor is followed by citrus and honey notes.

AGE: 17 years, 40%

NOSE: Dry and slightly peaty at first with warmer aromas of sherry

TASTE: A rich malt with sherry undertones and a peaty, dry finish.

AGE: 25 years, 40%

NOSE: A full, sweet malt with a rich aroma

TASTE: Oak tannins hover, while the overall taste is full-bodied and creamy with a smoky finish.

DRUMGUISH

DRUMGUISH DISTILLERY, GLEN YROMIE, KINGUSSIE, INVERNESS-SHIRE PH21 1NS
TEL: +44 (0) 1540 661060 FAX: +44 (0) 1540 661959

The story of Drumguish Distillery is the story of one family and, in particular, one man. The Christie family started to build Drumguish in 1962 near to the original distillery, which closed in 1911. Much of the work was carried out by George Christie himself and the building was completed in 1987. The new distillery produced its first spirit in December 1990. Drumguish is a hand-built stone building with an operational water wheel.

DISTILLERY FACTS

Highland		I wash I spirit
1990		N/A
River Tromie		No visitors

TASTING NOTES

AGE: Unaged, 40%

NOSE: A light aroma with hints of honey and fruit

TASTE: Soft on the palate with a little honey and a long, smooth finish.

DUFFTOWN

DUFFTOWN DISTILLERY, DUFFTOWN, KEITH, BANFFSHIRE AB55 4BR
TEL: +44 (0) 1340 820224 FAX: +44 (0) 1340 820060

The Dufftown-Glenlivet Distillery Co. was founded in 1896 when the distillery was built inside an old meal mill. In 1897 the distillery was taken over by P. Mackenzie & Co., owners of the Blair Athol Distillery. In 1933 the company was purchased by Arthur Bell & Sons. The number of stills was increased from two to four in 1967 and again from four to six in 1979.

DISTILLERY FACTS

Speyside		3 wash 3 spirit
1896		N/A
Jock's Well		No visitors

TASTING NOTES

AGE: 15 years, 43%

NOSE: Warm, fragrant

TASTE: Smooth, slightly sweet, with a hint of fruit.

THE EDRADOUR

EDRADOUR DISTILLERY, PITLOCHRY, PERTHSHIRE PH16 5JP
TEL: +44 (0) 1796 473524 FAX: +44 (0) 1796 472002

Edradour Distillery is Scotland's smallest. It was founded in 1825 on land rented from the Duke of Atholl, and is a good example of a working Victorian distillery.

In 1886 the distillery was acquired by William Whiteley & Co. Ltd., a subsidiary of J.G. Turney & Sons of the United States. Eventually it was bought by Campbell Distillers.

The Edradour is a golden, honey-colored malt.

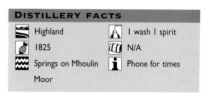

DISTILLERY FACTS

	Highland		1 wash 1 spirit
	1825		N/A
	Springs on Mhoulin Moor		Phone for times

TASTING NOTES

AGE: 10 years, 40%

NOSE: Delicate, sweet with a hint of peat

TASTE: Dry, slightly sweet with a nutty, smooth finish. A malt for any occasion.

GLENBURGIE

GLENBURGIE DISTILLERY, BY ALVES, FORRES, MORAYSHIRE IV36 0QY
TEL: +44 (0) 1343 850258 FAX: +44 (0) 1343 850480

Glenburgie Distillery was founded in 1810 as the Kilnflat Distillery and changed its name in 1871. In 1925 it was managed by Margaret Nicol, who is believed to have been the first female manager ever. In 1936 Glenburgie Distillery was purchased by Hiram Walker and eventually became part of Allied Distillers' portfolio. Glenburgie is situated at the foot of Mill Buie Hills above the village of Kinloss.

DISTILLERY FACTS

	Speyside		Mixture of ex-bourbon and some sherry
	1810		
	Local Springs		
	2 wash 2 spirit		No visitors

TASTING NOTES

AGE: 8 years, 40%

NOSE: Scent of herbs and fruit

TASTE: Strong at first with a lingering, warm, spicy finish.

GLEN DEVERON

MACDUFF DISTILLERY, BANFF, BANFFSHIRE AB4 3JT
TEL: +44 (0) 1261 812612 FAX: +44 (0) 1261 818083

The distillery was founded on the banks of the River Deveron in 1962 by a consortium and the company operated as Glen Deveron, which eventually became part of Bacardi Ltd. Macduff Distillery is the home of the Glen Deveron single malt whisky. If you buy Glen Deveron malt from the independent bottlers, however, the label will show the contents as Macduff single malt whisky.

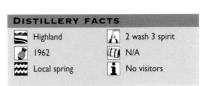

DISTILLERY FACTS

	Highland		2 wash 3 spirit
	1962		N/A
	Local spring		No visitors

TASTING NOTES

AGE: 12 years, 40%

NOSE: Delicate, fresh

TASTE: A medium-sweet malt with a long fresh finish.

THE GLENDRONACH

GLENDRONACH DISTILLERY, FORGUE, HUNTLY, ABERDEENSHIRE **AB54 6DA**
TEL: +44 (0) 1466 730202 FAX: +44 (0) 1466 730313

Distilling at The Glendronach was practiced illegally for many years and it was remote enough to avoid detection by the excisemen. In 1826, James Allardes and his associates were the second distillers to take out a license to distill whisky legally.

The distillery was purchased by William Teacher & Sons Ltd. in 1960. The Glendronach is a fine, deep, amber color and owes its character to the combination of in-house maltings, peat, and Highland water. The malt is distinctive, with some of the characteristics of a Speyside and others more closely associated with a Highland malt. In fact, some whisky writers place the Glendronach as being from the Highland region of Scotland.

DISTILLERY FACTS

〰	Speyside	𝄃𝄃𝄃	Seasoned oak and
🖐	1826		sherry
〰	Local Springs	ℹ	Tours and a shop.
🄰	2 wash 2 spirit		Phone for times

TASTING NOTES

AGE: 12 years, 40% Traditional

NOSE: Sweet, smooth aroma

TASTE: A long, sweet taste with smoky overtones and a pleasant finish.

GLENDULLAN

GLENDULLAN DISTILLERY, DUFFTOWN, KEITH, BANFFSHIRE AB55 4DJ
TEL: +44 (0) 1340 820250 FAX: +44 (0) 1340 820064

Glendullan Distillery was built in 1897. Initially it was owned by William Williams & Sons Ltd., blenders from Aberdeen. In 1919 the company was renamed Macdonald, Greenlees, & Williams, when Greenlees Brothers Ltd. took over the distillery. It was acquired by the Distillers Co. in 1926, was rebuilt in 1962, and a new distillery with six stills was added in 1972.

DISTILLERY FACTS

	Speyside		3 wash 3 spirit
	1897		N/A
	Springs in the Conval Hills		No visitors

TASTING NOTES

AGE: 12 years, 43%

NOSE: Delicate with a hint of almond

TASTE: A warm honey malt with a long finish.

GLEN ELGIN

GLEN ELGIN DISTILLERY, LONGMOR, ELGIN, MORAYSHIRE IV30 3SL
TEL +44 (0) 1343 860212 FAX: +44 (0) 1343 862077

Glen Elgin was designed by Charles Doig during the whisky boom of the 1890s. Production here began on May 1, 1900. The distillery was sold to the Glen Elgin-Glenlivet Distillery Co. Ltd. in 1901 and production ceased for a while. In 1906 it was bought by J. J. Blanche & Co. Ltd., but production continued to be inconsistent. In 1930 Glen Elgin was purchased by the Distillers Co.

DISTILLERY FACTS

	Speyside		4 wash 3 spirit
	1898–1900		N/A
	Local springs		No visitors

TASTING NOTES

AGE: No age, 43%

NOSE: Smoky aroma with a hint of honey

TASTE: Medium-bodied malt with a peaty taste, a hint of sweetness, and a long finish.

GLENFARCLAS

GLENFARCLAS DISTILLERY, BALLINDALLOCH, BANFFSHIRE **AB37 9BD**
TEL: +44 (0) 1807 500245 FAX: +44 (0) 1807 500234

A license was granted to Glenfarclas in 1836. In 1865 the distillery was purchased by John Grant, and, at the time of writing, it is still owned by the same family and is a truly independent malt whisky distillery.

Many of the original buildings have been modernized and the number of stills was increased from two to four in 1960 and to six in 1976. It has the largest stills and mash tun on Speyside.

The Glenfarclas visitor center has been fitted with original oak paneling

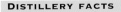

DISTILLERY FACTS

	Speyside		3 wash 3 spirit
	1836		Spanish oak
	Spring on Ben Rinnes		All year round. Phone for times

from an old passenger liner, once known as the *SS Empress* of Australia.

Malts are available in a variety of ages, from 10 to 30 years.

TASTING NOTES

AGE: 105, 60% (this cask-strength whisky is shown as unaged, but nothing is bottled at Glenfarclas until it is 10 years old)

NOSE: Very pungent with a round, ripe aroma

TASTE: A full sweet flavor with hints of caramel and a delicious aftertaste.

AGE: 25 years, 43%

NOSE: A warm aroma full of character and promise

TASTE: Its maturity is apparent immediately, and myriad flavors develop in the mouth. It has a long, slightly dry finish with oak undertones.

GLENFIDDICH

THE GLENFIDDICH DISTILLERY, DUFFTOWN, KEITH, BANFFSHIRE AB55 4DH
TEL: +44 (0) 1340 820373 FAX: +44 (0) 1340 820805

Glenfiddich was built by William Grant and his family—seven sons and two daughters—in 1886, and the first malt ran from the stills on Christmas Day in 1887. Whisky is still distilled there following traditional methods: for example, it still has its own cooperage with nine coopers repairing and preparing barrels.

Glenfiddich malt is produced unaged, but is at least eight years old. In 1963, Glenfiddich took the unusual step of marketing their whisky as a single malt in the U.K. and overseas, which was initially viewed with skepticism by other distillers, who continued to sell their malt to blenders but, thanks to this foresight, a market was created for single malts.

Glenfiddich Special Old Reserve single malt 40% is in a very distinctive

DISTILLERY FACTS

	Speyside		All oak—American bourbon of Spanish sherry
	1886		
	Robbie Dubh		
	5 wash 8 spirit— unusually small		Year-round. Phone for times— especially with groups of 12 or more

three-sided green bottle, and the malt is a pale golden color.

TASTING NOTES

AGE: Unaged, 40%

NOSE: A delicate, fresh aroma with a hint of peat

TASTE: Slightly dry at first with a fuller flavor developing, with subtle, sweet overtones.

GLEN GARIOCH

OLD MELDRUM, INVERURIE, ABERDEENSHIRE AB51 0ES
TEL: +44 (0) 1651 873450 FAX: +44 (0) 1651 872578

Records show that Glen Garioch was founded by Thomas Simpson in 1798, but Simpson was thought to be producing spirit in 1785, whether or not at Glen Garioch is unclear. The distillery was purchased by several companies until it was closed in 1968. In 1970, Stanley P. Morrison (Agencies) Ltd. acquired the distillery and increased the number of stills to four.

Floor maltings were an important part of the distillation process at Glen Garioch, which was mothballed in 1995.

The malt is available in various ages and ranges in color, from pale gold to golden copper.

DISTILLERY FACTS

	Highland		Ex-bourbon and
	1798		sherry (bottled
	Springs on Percock Hill		strength varies with age)
	2 wash 2 spirit		No visitors

TASTING NOTES

AGE: Unaged, 40%

NOSE: Soft hint of peat and orange blossom

TASTE: Peaty at first, then overtones of fruit and honey with a long crisp finish.

AGE: 15 years, 43%

NOSE: Warmer, fruitier aroma with hints of oak

TASTE: Warm and glowing with citrus and smoke, and a long mellow finish.

AGE: 21 years, 43%

NOSE: Honey and peat with a slight hint of chocolate

TASTE: Full-bodied, sweeter with a hint of smoke and a warm mellow finish.

GLENGOYNE

GLENGOYNE DISTILLERY, DUMGOYNE, STIRLINGSHIRE G63 9LB
TEL: +44 (0) 1360 550229 FAX: +44 (0) 1360 550094

A license was issued to Burnfoot Distillery in 1833 and leased to George Connell. In 1851–67 the distillery belonged to John McLelland and was then taken over by Archibald C. McLellan, who sold it to Lang Brothers. It was then renamed Glen Guin, and the name was changed to Glengoyne in 1905.

Glengoyne became part of Robertson & Baxter in 1965 and the distillery was rebuilt a year later. Glengoyne is situated on the West Highland Way which makes a good stopping off point for ramblers going from Fort William to Glasgow.

Glengoyne single malt whisky is a pale, white wine-colored malt made from unpeated barley.

DISTILLERY FACTS

	Highland		Ex-sherry and refill
	1833	i	Phone for times.
	Burn from Campsie Hills		Recommended by Scottish Tourist Board
	1 wash 2 spirit		

TASTING NOTES

AGE: 10 years, 40%

NOSE: A clean, sunny, floral aroma

TASTE: Medium-bodied malt with hints of honey and a slight hint of fruit.

GLEN GRANT

GLEN GRANT DISTILLERY, ROTHES, MORAYSHIRE AB38 7BS
TEL: +44 (0) 1542 783318 FAX: +44 (0) 1542 783306

Glen Grant was founded by John and James Grant in 1840. After their deaths, Major James Grant, James's son, ran the distillery for almost 60 years.

In 1931 the distillery was inherited by Major Grant's grandson, Douglas Mackessack, who built up Glen Grant to the internationally renowned brand it is today. In 1961 Giovinetti took 50 cases of Glen Grant 5-years-old back with him to Milan. Today, Glen Grant is the number one brand of whisky in Italy.

DISTILLERY FACTS

	Speyside		4 wash 4 spirit
	1840		N/A
	The Caperdonich Well		Mar.–Oct. Phone for times

TASTING NOTES

AGE: Unaged, 40%

NOSE: Dry, slightly tangy

TASTE: A light, dry malt with a faint hint of fruit in the finish.

GLEN KEITH

GLEN KEITH DISTILLERY, STATION ROAD, KEITH, BANFFSHIRE AB55 3BU
TEL: +44 (0) 1542 783042 FAX: +44 (0) 1542 783055

One of the first new distilleries to open in the twentieth century, Glen Keith was built on the site of a corn mill in 1958. It was originally built with three stills for triple distillation. In 1970 the first gas-fired still in Scotland was installed here. Glen Keith is used in fine, blended whiskies, including Passport. Visitors to Glen Keith Distillery can see an audio-visual tape entitled "Passport Experience" which tells the history of the blend.

DISTILLERY FACTS

	Speyside		3 wash 3 spirit
	1958		N/A
	Balloch Hill springs		Phone for appointment

TASTING NOTES

AGE: 1983, 43%

NOSE: Warm, scented with hints of oak and peat

TASTE: A delicate malt with fruit and a hint of caramel and a long medium finish.

GLENKINCHIE

GLENKINCHIE DISTILLERY, PENTCAITLAND, EAST LOTHIAN EH34 5ET
TEL: +44 (0) 1875 340333 FAX: +44 (0) 1875 342007

Glenkinchie was founded in 1837 by John and George Rate. Production ceased in 1853, and in 1880 the distillery was reinstated by a group of businessmen. In 1890 Glenkinchie Distillery Co. Ltd. was formed. The company continued until 1914, when it became part of Scottish Malt Distillers Ltd. In 1968 it ceased to malt its own barley, and the Museum of Malt Whisky Production is housed inside the old malting facilities.

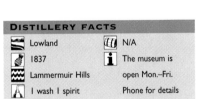

DISTILLERY FACTS

	Lowland		N/A
	1837		The museum is open Mon.–Fri.
	Lammermuir Hills		Phone for details
	1 wash 1 spirit		

TASTING NOTES

AGE: 10 years, 43%

NOSE: Orange blossom and honey

TASTE: A smooth, light malt with a rounded flavor, and a hint of sweetness and smoke, with a long finish.

THE GLENLIVET

THE GLENLIVET DISTILLERY, BALLINDALLOCH, BANFFSHIRE AB37 9DB
TEL: +44 (0) 1542 783220 FAX: +44 (0) 1542 783218

The Glenlivet was the first distillery to take out a license under the 1823 Act of Parliament designed to set a basis for taxation so that legal distilling was economically worthwhile. The Glenlivet was founded by George Smith in 1824 at Upper Drumin Farm. At first he had to fend off his neighbors—illegal distillers who tried to burn the distillery down. But, with the help of a pair of hair-trigger pistols, he managed to persuade them to leave him alone. These pistols are proudly displayed in the Glenlivet reception center.

In 1858 Smith was joined by his son John, and a new distillery was built at Minmore Farm. The Glenlivet remained in the Smith family until 1975, when the owner, Captain Bill Smith, died. In 1977 the company was purchased by the Seagram Co. Ltd.

DISTILLERY FACTS

	Speyside		N/A
	1824		Mid-Mar.–end Oct.
	Josie's Well		Phone for times.
	4 wash 4 spirit		Admission charge

TASTING NOTES

AGE: 12 years, 40%

NOSE: A fragrant malt with hints of fruit

TASTE: A medium body and a sweet, slightly sherry taste with a long finish.

AGE: 18 years, 43%

NOSE: A rich aroma with caramel and peat

TASTE: A gloriously rich malt, yet dry, with fruit, peat, and a spicy, sweet finish.

GLENLOSSIE

GLENLOSSIE DISTILLERY, ELGIN, MORAYSHIRE IV30 3SS
TEL: +44 (0) 1343 860331 FAX: +44 (0) 1343 860302

Glenlossie is situated near Elgin, a town synonymous with whisky, and is adjacent to Mannochmore. Glenlossie Distillery was founded in 1876 by John Duff with John Hopkins, who ceased to work in 1888. A new company was formed, the Glenlossie-Glenlivet Distillery, which was then taken over by Scottish Malt Distillers in 1919.

In 1962, the number of stills was increased from four to six. The spirit stills have purifiers just between the lyne arms and condensers, which add something different to this light, fresh malt with a light lemon-gold color.

DISTILLERY FACTS

≋	Speyside	◭	3 wash 3 spirit
🌾	1976	🗒	N/A
〰	The Bardon Burn	ℹ	No visitors

TASTING NOTES

AGE: 10 years, 43%

NOSE: A light, fresh aroma with a delightful hint of honey and spice

TASTE: Smooth with honey, smoke, and a little oak.

GLENMORANGIE

GLENMORANGIE DISTILLERY, TAIN, ROSS-SHIRE IV19 1PZ
TEL: +44 (0) 1862 892043 FAX: +44 (0) 1862 893862

The distillery was first licensed in 1843 by William Mathieson, and the first spirit was distilled in 1849. The first sales of Glenmorangie were made overseas in 1880. In 1887 the company was reconstructed as the Glenmorangie Distillery Co. Ltd. and in 1920 was bought by Macdonald and Muir. The distillery was rebuilt in 1979 and the number of stills doubled to four.

In 1996 the new Wood Finish Range was launched as a special presentation to celebrate the 80th birthday of the

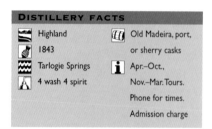

DISTILLERY FACTS	
Highland	Old Madeira, port, or sherry casks
1843	
Tarlogie Springs	Apr.–Oct., Nov.–Mar. Tours.
4 wash 4 spirit	Phone for times. Admission charge

former British Prime Minister, Sir Edward Heath. These malts are well worth seeking out.

The malts vary in color from golden honey to golden amber to a beautiful copper with rose and gold.

TASTING NOTES

AGE: Madeira Wood Finish, 12 years, 43%

NOSE: Fresh, sweet, slightly nutty with citrus

TASTE: Spicy with hints of citrus and honey, with a dry finish.

AGE: Port Wood Finish, 12 years, 43%

NOSE: Warm caramel, yet fresh

TASTE: Gloriously full and smooth on the mouth with hints of citrus and spice.

AGE: Sherry Wood Finish, 12 years, 43%

NOSE: Sherry with malt and honey

TASTE: Full-bodied with sherry and spice, with a long, flavorful finish.

GLEN MORAY

GLEN MORAY DISTILLERY, ELGIN, MORAYSHIRE IV30 1YE
TEL: +44 (0) 1343 542577 FAX: +44 (0) 1343 546195

Glen Moray is in the middle of one of the best farming areas of Scotland. It began as a brewery and was converted in 1897 by the Glen Moray Glenlivet Distillery Co. Ltd.

The distillery closed in 1910 and was reopened by Macdonald and Muir Ltd. in 1923. There is a sense of timelessness and the distillery still looks reminiscent of a Highland farm, constructed with buildings around a courtyard.

DISTILLERY FACTS

	Speyside		2 wash 2 spirit
	1897		N/A
	River Lossie		Phone for appointment

TASTING NOTES

AGE: Glen Moray, 12 years, 40%

NOSE: Delicate, with hints of summer

TASTE: A medium-bodied malt with a hint of peat and a warm, slightly sweet finish. A good after-dinner malt.

GLEN ORD

GLEN ORD DISTILLERY, MUIR OF ORD, ROSS-SHIRE IV6 7UJ
TEL: +44 (0) 1463 871421 FAX: +44 (0) 1463 872008

Glen Ord Distillery was founded in 1838 by Robert Johnstone and Donald McLennan in an area renowned for whisky distilling. There were nine other small stills, all licensed. In 1860, Ord was acquired by Alexander McLennan, who was then declared bankrupt in 1871. It passed to his widow, who eventually married Alexander McKenzie. He ran the business until 1887, when James Watson & Co., blenders of Dundee, purchased Glen Ord Distillery.

Traditional maltings ceased in 1961 and a Saladin-box system was introduced.

DISTILLERY FACTS

~	Highland	A	3 wash 3 spirit
🌾	1838	🛢	N/A
~~	Lochs Nan Eun and Nan Bonnach	i	Mon.–Fri. Phone for times

TASTING NOTES

AGE: 12 years, 40%

NOSE: Full-bodied, warm, spicy

TASTE: Flavorful with caramel, nutmeg, and a long, smooth finish.

Glen Ord became part of the Distillers Co. in 1925. Much of the distillery was rebuilt in 1966.

GLENROTHES

GLENROTHES DISTILLERY, ROTHES, MORAYSHIRE AB38 7AA
TEL: +44 (0) 1340 872300 FAX: +44 (0) 1340 872172

Glenrothes Distillery was built by W. Grant & Co. beside the Burn of Rothes, which flows from the Mannoch Hills, in 1878, and production started in December 1979. In 1887, the distillery and the Islay Distillery Company amalgamated to form the Highland Distilleries Co. Ltd. The water supply comes from The Lady's Well. Records show that this was where the only daughter of a fourteenth-century Earl of Rothes was murdered by the "Wolf of Badenoch" while attempting to save her lover's life.

Extensive work was carried out on the distillery in 1896. In 1963 the number of stills was increased from four to six, and in 1980 from six to ten.

DISTILLERY FACTS

Speyside	Varying mix of
1878	refills, sherry, and
The Lady's Well	ex-bourbon
5 wash 5 spirit	Invitation only

TASTING NOTES

AGE: 1972, 43%

NOSE: Full caramel with spice

TASTE: Full-bodied with warm oak and honey notes and a long, rich, sweet finish.

AGE: 1979, 43%

NOSE: Warm caramel with faint undertones of chocolate

TASTE: Medium-bodied, flavorful malt with hints of toffee and orange in the mouth, and a long honey and citrus finish.

AGE: 1982, 43%

NOSE: Warm caramel nose

TASTE: Full-bodied with toffee and vanilla with a long flavorful finish.

AGE: 1984, 43%

NOSE: Fine sherry, vanilla, and malt aroma

TASTE: Smooth, medium-bodied with tropical fruit and malt flavors and a long, smooth finish.

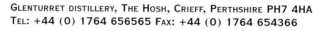

GLENTURRET

GLENTURRET DISTILLERY, THE HOSH, CRIEFF, PERTHSHIRE PH7 4HA
TEL: +44 (0) 1764 656565 FAX: +44 (0) 1764 654366

Built in 1775, this is Scotland's oldest Highland malt whisky distillery. Research shows that distilling began in this area in 1717. This is one of the smallest distilleries in Scotland, and more than 190,000 visitors each year pay a visit.

DISTILLERY FACTS

〰️	Highland	🎇	Mix of bourbon
🌿	1775		and sherry oak
〰️	Loch Turret	ℹ️	Phone for times
⛺	1 wash 1 spirit		

TASTING NOTES

AGE: 12 years, 40%

NOSE: Aromatic, hints of sherry and caramel

TASTE: A full-bodied malt with warming flavor and a long, satisfying finish.

AGE: 15 years, 40%

NOSE: Crisp, fresh yet sweet

TASTE: Full flavor with angelica and spice, with a long, fruity finish.

HIGHLAND PARK

HIGHLAND PARK DISTILLERY, HOLM ROAD, KIRKWALL, ORKNEY KW15 1SU
TEL: +44 (0) 1856 873107 FAX: +44 (0) 1856 876091

This is the northernmost distillery in Scotland, situated on the island of Orkney. It is reputed to have been founded by David Robertson and passed through various hands until the stills, a malt barn, and other buildings were purchased by Robert Borwick in 1826. In 1898 the number of stills was doubled to four. The distillery was bought by Highland Distilleries in 1935. Highland Park is a glorious deep gold color.

DISTILLERY FACTS

〰️	Highland–Orkney	⛺	2 wash 2 spirit
🌿	1798	🎇	Mix of sherry and
〰️	Springs from Cattie		bourbon oak casks
	Maggie's pool	ℹ️	Phone for times

TASTING NOTES

AGE: 12 years, 40%

NOSE: Rich, smoky, with a hint of honey

TASTE: Gloriously rounded with heathery, peaty, and warm, nutty overtones and a dry yet sweet aftertaste.

INCHGOWER

INCHGOWER DISTILLERY, BUCKIE, BANFFSHIRE AB56 2AB
TEL: +44 (0) 1542 831161 FAX: +44 (0) 1542 834531

Inchgower Distillery was built in 1872 by Alexander Wilson to replace Tochineal Distillery, which had been founded, also by Wilson, in 1832. Inchgower went into liquidation in 1930 and in 1936 Buckie Council purchased the distillery for the equivalent of $1,600. Arthur Bell & Sons Ltd. bought it in 1938 and the number of stills was increased from two to four in 1966. It eventually became part of Distillers Co.

Buckie is situated near the mouth of the River Spey, and a bottle of Inchgower single malt whisky shows an oyster-catcher on the label.

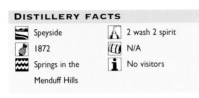

DISTILLERY FACTS

🏴	Speyside	🅰	2 wash 2 spirit
🌾	1872	🛢	N/A
〰	Springs in the Menduff Hills	ℹ	No visitors

TASTING NOTES

AGE: 14 years, 43%

NOSE: Sweet, with a hint of apple

TASTE: Medium-bodied malt with spice and a light, sweet finish.

INCHMURRIN

LOCK LOMOND DISTILLERY, ALEXANDRIA, DUMBARTONSHIRE G83 0TL
TEL: +44 (0) 1389 752781 FAX: +44 (0) 1389 757977

Inchmurrin Distillery was founded in 1966 by the Littlemill Distillery Co. Ltd., which was a joint venture between Duncan Thomas and Barton Brands of the United States. Two types of single malt were produced by Littlemill: Inchmurrin and Rosdhu. In 1971, Barton Brands took over the company, and built new blending and bottling facilities, but in 1984 the distillery closed. Inchmurrin reopened in 1987.

DISTILLERY FACTS

	Highland		2 wash 2 spirit
	1966		N/A
	Loch Lomond		No visitors

TASTING NOTES

AGE: 10 years, 40%

NOSE: Malty, spicy

TASTE: A light-bodied, spicy malt with a hint of lemon and a short finish.

ISLE OF JURA

ISLE OF JURA DISTILLERY, CRAIGHOUSE, JURA, ARGYLLSHIRE PA60 7XT
TEL: +44 (0) 1496 820240 FAX: +44 (0) 1496 820344

Jura is one of the least populated islands with only about 200 inhabitants. The distillery is one of the main employers. It is believed that Jura's isolation encouraged illegal distilling and that whisky has been produced here since the late sixteenth century. Jura was founded in 1810. Since then there have been various owners and some periods of inactivity. The distillery now forms part of the Whyte & Mackay portfolio.

DISTILLERY FACTS

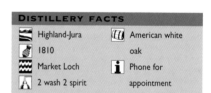

	Highland-Jura		American white
	1810		oak
	Market Loch		Phone for
	2 wash 2 spirit		appointment

TASTING NOTES

AGE: 10 years, 40%

NOSE: A golden malt with a peaty aroma

TASTE: A light malt, suitable as an aperitif, yet with a full flavor and undertones of honey and smoke.

KNOCKANDO

KNOCKANDO DISTILLERY, KNOCKANDO, MORAYSHIRE AB38 7RT
TEL: +44 (0) 1340 810205 FAX: +44 (0) 1340 810369

Knockando is Gaelic for "little black hill." The distillery, built on the banks of the Spey in 1898, was founded by the Knockando-Glenlivet Distillery Co., and transferred to J. Thomson & Co. in 1900. It was purchased by W.A. Gilbey Ltd. in 1904 and eventually became part of International Distillers & Vintners Ltd. The distillery was rebuilt in 1969 and the number of stills was doubled to four. It is a pure golden-colored single malt.

DISTILLERY FACTS

Speyside		Ex-bourbon and
1898		sherry
Cardnach Spring		Phone for
2 wash 2 spirit		appointment

TASTING NOTES

AGE: Distilled 1982, bottled 1996, 40%

NOSE: Fragrant, spicy

TASTE: A syrup-flavored malt with undertones of spice, vanilla, and filbert.

LAGAVULIN

LAGAVULIN DISTILLERY, PORT ELLEN, ISLAY, ARGYLL PA42 7DZ
TEL: +44 (0) 1496 302400 FAX: +44 (0) 1496 302321

Originally there were two distilleries here: one built in 1816 by John Johnston and one built in 1817 by Archibald Campbell. Campbell stopped distilling in 1821 and John Johnston occupied both distilleries from 1825 to 1834. In 1837 there was only one distillery, owned by Donald Johnston. It was acquired by John Graham in 1852 and, after various changes of ownership, Langavulin became part of the Distillers Co.

DISTILLERY FACTS

Islay		N/A
1816		Call +44 (0) 1496
Solum Lochs		302250 for an
2 wash 2 spirit		appointment

TASTING NOTES

AGE: 16 years, 43%

NOSE: Very powerful, peaty

TASTE: Full-bodied, pungent peat flavor with undertones of sweetness and a long finish.

LAPHROAIG

LAPHROAIG DISTILLERY, PORT ELLEN, ISLE OF ISLAY PA42 7DU
TEL: +44 (0) 1496 302418 FAX: +44 (0) 1496 302496

Laphroaig Distillery was founded in 1815 by Alexander and Donald Johnston, who started farming at Laphroaig around 1810. The distillery remained in family ownership until 1908, when the proprietor, Ian Hunter, left it to a Bessie Williamson, the first woman to run a malt whisky distillery in Scotland entirely on her own. Laphroaig has a distinctive flavor. During Prohibition it was legally imported to the U.S. because of its unique "medicinal" characteristics. Eventually, Laphroaig became part of the Allied Distillers' malt whisky portfolio.

Laphroaig is one of the few distillers to malt barley in house. It is dried over fire kilns that burn local peat. Laphroaig is a vibrant gold malt.

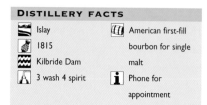

DISTILLERY FACTS

	Islay		American first-fill
	1815		bourbon for single
	Kilbride Dam		malt
	3 wash 4 spirit		Phone for appointment

TASTING NOTES

AGE: 10 years, 40%

NOSE: Instantly recognizable, full, peaty, slightly medicinal

TASTE: A full-bodied malt with an initial peaty flavor, which develops to a touch of sweetness. A long, dry, slightly salty finish.

LINKWOOD

LINKWOOD DISTILLERY, ELGIN, MORAYSHIRE IV30 3RD
TEL: +44 (0) 1343 547004 FAX: +44 (0) 1343 549449

Linkwood Distillery was founded in 1825 by Peter Brown, agent for Seafield Estates in Moray and Banffshire. His father farmed at Linkwood and it is likely that much of the barley came from the farm. In 1872 the distillery was rebuilt by his son, William. In 1897 the company was floated as the Linkwood-Glenlivet Distillery Co. Ltd., which was acquired by Scottish Malt Distillers. The number of stills was increased to six in 1971.

DISTILLERY FACTS

	Speyside		3 wash 3 spirit
	1825		N/A
	Springs near Millbuies Loch		By appointment only

TASTING NOTES

AGE: 20 years, distilled 1972, 58.4%

NOSE: Full-bodied with fruit and caramel

TASTE: Full-bodied malt with honey and a hint of peat and a long, sweet finish.

LONGMORN

LONGMORN DISTILLERY, NEAR ELGIN, MORAYSHIRE IV30 3SJ
TEL: +44 (0) 1542 783400 FAX: +44 (0) 1542 783404

Longmorn Distillery was built in 1894 by Shirres, Thomson, and Duff, and the first distillation was produced in December of that year. In 1898, John Duff ran into financial trouble so Hill, Thomson, & Co. Ltd. and the manager, James Grant, continued to run the distillery until 1970, when the company merged with the Glenlivet and Glen Grant Distillers Ltd. It was eventually acquired by the Seagram Co. Ltd.

DISTILLERY FACTS

	Speyside		N/A
	1894		By appointment only
	Local springs		
	4 wash 4 spirit		

TASTING NOTES

AGE: 15 years, 43%

NOSE: Fragrant, delicate, slightly fruity

TASTE: Full of flavor with hints of fruit, flowers, and filberts, with a long, sweet finish.

THE MACALLAN

THE MACALLAN DISTILLERY, CRAIGELLACHIE, BANFFSHIRE **AB38 9RX**
TEL: +44 (0) 1340 871471 FAX: +44 (0) 1340 871212

The Macallan Distillery was founded in 1824 by Alexander Reid at the site of a ford across the River Spey at Easter Elchies. After several changes of owner, the distillery was bought by Roderick Kemp in 1892, and he renamed it Macallan-Glenlivet. It remained in the Kemp family until 1996, when it became part of the Highland Distilleries malt whisky portfolio.

The number of stills was increased from six to 12 in 1965, and to 18 in 1974, and finally, in 1975, to 21. The Macallan is matured in old oak sherry casks, which impart a special flavor.

DISTILLERY FACTS

	Speyside		Ex-sherry oak
	1824		(bottled strength
	The Ringorm Burn		varies by age)
	7 wash 14 spirit		By appointment only

TASTING NOTES

AGE: 10 years, 40%

NOSE: Light, fragrant sherry

TASTE: Full-bodied sherry with hints of vanilla and fruit, and a long, smooth, well-rounded finish.

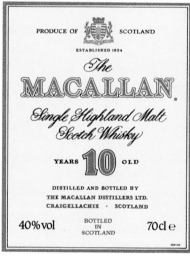

PRODUCE OF SCOTLAND

ESTABLISHED 1824

The

MACALLAN

Single Highland Malt
Scotch Whisky

YEARS **10** OLD

DISTILLED AND BOTTLED BY
THE MACALLAN DISTILLERS LTD.
CRAIGELLACHIE · SCOTLAND

40% vol | BOTTLED IN SCOTLAND | 70cl e

MANNOCHMORE

MANNOCHMORE DISTILLERY, ELGIN, MORAYSHIRE IV30 3SS
TEL: +44 (0) 1343 860331 FAX: +44 (0) 1343 860302

Mannochmore 12-year-old single malt has a drawing of a great spotted woodpecker on the label, an inhabitant of the Millbuies Woods, which are next to the distillery. Mannochmore was founded in 1971 and was built alongside Glenlossie Distillery.

Mannochmore was closed in 1985, but United Distillers reopened the distillery in 1989. It was mothballed again in 1995, but could yet be revived.

Mannochmore single malt is a beautiful pale, gold color.

DISTILLERY FACTS

🏴	Speyside	Ⓐ	3 wash 3 spirit
🍍	1971	🛢	N/A
〰	The Bardon Burn	ℹ	No visitors

TASTING NOTES

AGE: 12 years, 43%

NOSE: Delicate, springlike, with a hint of peat

TASTE: A fine malt with a clean, fresh taste and a lingering, slightly sweet aftertaste.

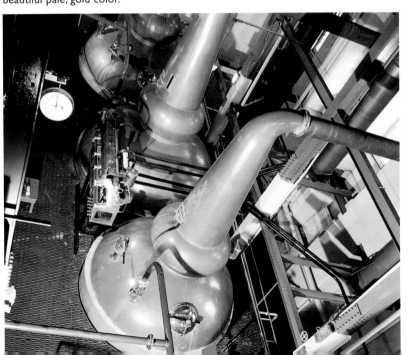

MILTONDUFF

MILTONDUFF DISTILLERY, MILTONDUFF, ELGIN, MORAYSHIRE IV30 3TQ
TEL: +44 (0) 1343 547433 FAX: +44 (0) 1343 548802

The Miltonduff Distillery is in the Glen of Pluscarden on the site of the Pluscarden Priory on the banks of the Black Burn. It was one of the first distilleries to take out a license in 1824.

History relates that there were more than 50 illegal distilleries on the same site and that smuggling continued well into the nineteenth century. The Glen of Pluscarden was an ideal spot for illegal distilling as the surrounding hills form a triangle, which enabled the smugglers to devise a signal system.

The distillery was eventually acquired by Allied Distillers as the largest malt distillery in its portfolio. Most of the distillery's production goes into the blending of Ballantine's Whisky.

DISTILLERY FACTS

	Speyside		Usually ex-bourbon
	1824		By appointment
	Black Burn		only
	3 wash 3 spirit		

TASTING NOTES

AGE: 12 years, 43%

NOSE: Fragrant

TASTE: A medium-bodied malt with a fresh flavor.

MIYAGIKYO

SENDAI MIYAGIKYO DISTILLERY, NIKKA 1-BANCHI, AOBA-KU, SENDAI-SHI, MIYAGI-KEN 989034, JAPAN
TEL: +81 (0) 22 378 7532 FAX: +81 (0) 22 395 2861

In 1918, Masataka Taketsuru, the son of a sake brewery owner, went to Glasgow University to learn about whisky, and returned to Japan and set up two distilleries. The first was in Yoichi, Hokkaido, the most northern part of Japan, in 1934. Sendai, the second distillery, was built in 1969 to the north of the main island, and produces Miyagikyo, a mahogany-colored single malt.

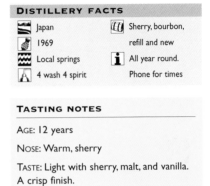

DISTILLERY FACTS

	Japan		Sherry, bourbon, refill and new
	1969		All year round.
	Local springs		Phone for times
	4 wash 4 spirit		

TASTING NOTES

AGE: 12 years

NOSE: Warm, sherry

TASTE: Light with sherry, malt, and vanilla. A crisp finish.

MORTLACH

MORTLACH DISTILLERY, DUFFTOWN, KEITH, BANFFSHIRE AB55 4AQ
TEL: +44 (0) 1340 820318 FAX: +44 (0) 1340 820019

Mortlach Distillery was founded in 1824 by James Findlater, Donald Mackintosh, and Alexander Gordon. It was acquired in 1832 by A. & T. Gregory, who sold it to J. & J. Grant of Glen Grant Distillery. George Cowie joined the company in 1854 and the distillery remained in his family's ownership until 1897, when it was purchased by John Walker & Sons Ltd. It was rebuilt in 1963 and became part of the Distillers Co. in 1924.

DISTILLERY FACTS

	Speyside		3 wash 3 spirit
	1824		N/A
	Springs in the Conval Hills		No visitors

TASTING NOTES

AGE: 16 years, 43%

NOSE: Fruity, warm, with a hint of peat

TASTE: Full-bodied with caramel and spice and a long, sherry and honey finish.

OBAN

OBAN DISTILLERY, STAFFORD STREET, OBAN, ARGYLL PA34 5NH
TEL: +44 (0) 1631 562110 FAX: +44 (0) 1631 563344

Oban was founded in 1794 by the Stevensons, who were local businessmen. It remained in their hands until 1866, when it was purchased by Peter Cumstie, a local merchant. Walter Higgin purchased Oban in 1883, and rebuilt the distillery, and in 1898 Higgin sold it to the Oban and Aultmore-Glenlivet Distilleries Ltd. The buildings at Oban have remained virtually unchanged for nearly 100 years.

DISTILLERY FACTS			
	Highland		1 wash 1 spirit
	1794		N/A
	Loch Gleann a'Bhearriadh		Year round. Phone for times

TASTING NOTES

AGE: 14 years, 43%

NOSE: Light with a hint of peat

TASTE: Medium-bodied malt with a hint of smoke and a long finish.

OLD FETTERCAIRN

FETTERCAIRN, DISTILLERY ROAD, LAURENCEKIRK, KINCARDINESHIRE AB30 1YE
TEL: +44 (0) 1561 340244 FAX: +44 (0) 1561 340447

This distillery was built in 1824 by Sir Alexander Ramsay. The building was originally a corn mill, which was destroyed by fire in 1887, but was soon reconstructed. In 1966 the distillery was expanded, doubling the number of stills to four. After several changes of ownership, Old Fettercairn was purchased by the Tomintoul Glenlivet Distillery Co. Ltd. in 1971 and eventually became part of the Whyte and Mackay Group.

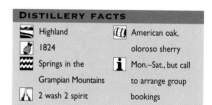

DISTILLERY FACTS			
	Highland		American oak,
	1824		oloroso sherry
	Springs in the Grampian Mountains		Mon.–Sat., but call to arrange group
	2 wash 2 spirit		bookings

TASTING NOTES

AGE: 10 years, 43%

NOSE: Delicate, fresh with a hint of smoke

TASTE: A good introductory malt with a full flavor, undertones of peat, and a dry finish.

ROYAL BRACKLA

ROYAL BRACKLA DISTILLERY, CAWDOR, NAIRN, NAIRNSHIRE IV12 5QY
TEL: +44 (0) 1667 404280 FAX: +44 (0) 1667 404743

This distillery was granted the Royal Warrant in 1833 by King William IV, and its single malt is marketed as "The King's Own Whisky." Brackla was founded in 1812 by Captain William Fraser. Robert Fraser took over in 1852, and the distillery continued in his name until 1898, when it was sold to John Mitchell and James Leict of Aberdeen. Brackla was sold to Scottish Malt Distillers in 1943.

DISTILLERY FACTS

	Highland		2 wash 2 spirit
	1812		N/A
	The Cawdor Burn		No visitors

TASTING NOTES

AGE: Unaged, 40%

NOSE: Peat, honey, and spice

TASTE: A medium-bodied malt with a spicy sweetness and a clean, slightly fruity finish.

ROYAL LOCHNAGAR

ROYAL LOCHNAGAR, CRATHIE, BALLATER, ABERDEENSHIRE AB35 5TB
TEL: +44 (0) 1339 742273 FAX: +44 (0) 1339 742312

There were once two Lochnagars, but this one was established in 1845 by John Begg, a farmer. In 1848 Begg invited Queen Victoria to visit the distillery and she did, hence the word *Royal* in the name. The distillery is situated close to Balmoral in the beautiful Deeside countryside and even today looks very much like a cluster of farm buildings. Royal Lochnagar eventually became part of the United Distillers malt whisky portfolio.

DISTILLERY FACTS

	Highland		N/A
	1845		Easter–Oct.,
	Local springs		Nov.–Easter. Phone
	1 wash 1 spirit		for times.
			Restaurant

TASTING NOTES

AGE: 12 years, 40%

NOSE: Warm, spicy aroma

TASTE: Fruit, malt, and a hint of vanilla and oak. Sweet, long-lasting finish.

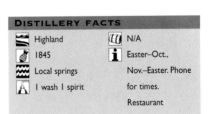

SCAPA

SCAPA DISTILLERY, ST OLA, ORKNEY KW15 1SE
TEL: +44 (0) 1856 872071 FAX: +44 (0) 1856 876585

Scapa is one of Scotland's northernmost distilleries, on the banks of the Lingro Burn on the island of Orkney. It passed through many owners until the early 1950s, when Hiram Walker of Allied Distillers bought it from Bloch Bros. of Glasgow. The distillery was rebuilt in 1959 and was mothballed in 1993. A new Scapa 12-year-old single malt is bottled by Allied Distillers Ltd. Other ages can be obtained from Gordon & MacPhail.

DISTILLERY FACTS

	Highland–Orkney		1 wash 1 spirit
	1885		Ex-bourbon
	Springs		Phone for appointment

TASTING NOTES

AGE: 12 years, 40%

NOSE: Sea, peat, and heather

TASTE: Mix of salt and citrus with a long-lasting, crisp finish.

SINGLETON

SINGLETON AUCHROISK DISTILLERY, MULBEN, BANFFSHIRE AB55 3XS
TEL: +44 (0) 1542 860333 FAX: +44 (0) 1542 860265

A relative newcomer, Singleton Distillery was founded in 1974, and The Singleton was first marketed in the U.K. as a single malt whisky in 1978. It was opened by International Distillers and Vintners Ltd., which passed management to its subsidiary, Justerini & Brooks Ltd.

This malt is available at various ages. At 10 years old, 43%, The Singleton has a color similar to beech leaves in the fall.

DISTILLERY FACTS

	Speyside		Ex-bourbon and sherry
	1974		
	Dorie's Well		Phone for appointment
	4 wash 4 spirit		

TASTING NOTES

AGE: 10 years, 43%

NOSE: Rich, warming, with sherry notes

TASTE: Full flavor, hints of tangerine and honey; deliciously smooth with a warm, long finish.

SPEYBURN

SPEYBURN DISTILLERY, ROTHES, ABERLOUR, MORAYSHIRE AB38 7AG
TEL: +44 (0) 1340 831231 FAX: +44 (0) 1340 831678

Speyburn Distillery was founded in 1897 by John Hopkins & Co., and nestles in the picturesque rolling hills of the Spey Valley. Tradition has it that distilling began before the building work had been completed, and it was so cold that employees had to work in their overcoats. Speyburn was acquired by the Distillers Co. in 1916 and in 1992 was purchased by Inver House Distillers Ltd. Speyburn is a pale gold color reminiscent of larch trees in winter.

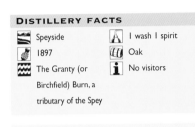

DISTILLERY FACTS

	Speyside		1 wash 1 spirit
	1897		Oak
	The Granty (or Birchfield) Burn, a tributary of the Spey		No visitors

TASTING NOTES

AGE: 10 years, 40%

NOSE: A dry, sweet-scented aroma

TASTE: Warm and flavorful with hints of honey and a herbal finish.

SPRINGBANK

SPRINGBANK DISTILLERY, CAMPBELTOWN, ARGYLL PA28 6EJ
TEL: +44 (0) 1586 552085 FAX: +44 (0) 1586 553215

Springbank was built in 1828 by two brothers, Archibald and Hugh Mitchell. By 1872 they owned four distilleries in the area. Production of a single malt whisky at Springbank is entirely self-contained. From the very first stage of malting barley in the traditional way to the final step of bottling, everything is done on site. Springbank is one of only two distilleries to bottle at source—the other is Glenfiddich.

DISTILLERY FACTS

	Campbeltown		Refill whisky, ex-bourbon, and sherry
	1828		Phone for appointment
	Crosshill Loch		
	2 wash 2 spirit		

TASTING NOTES

AGE: 15 years, 46%

NOSE: Fresh, rich with a hint of peat

TASTE: Medium-bodied with an initial sweetness followed by a taste of the sea and oak.

STRATHISLA

STRATHISLA DISTILLERY, SEAFIELD AVENUE, KEITH, BANFFSHIRE AB55 3BS
TEL: +44 (0) 1542 783042

Strathisla was founded by George Taylor and Alexander Milne in 1786 as the Milltown Distillery. At that time the town of Keith was renowned for its linen mills. The distillery was then managed by several local businessmen and in 1830 was purchased by William Longmore, a local merchant. In 1882, he died, and the company was floated as William Longmore & Co. Ltd. But around this time the name was changed to Strathisla, and major construction work was carried out, including rebuilding the kiln with pagodas.

In 1946 Longmore became a private company under the management of George Pomeroy, who was found guilty of tax evasion. The company was closed in 1949, but was sold to Chivas Brothers in 1950. Strathisla is a warm coppery-gold single malt.

DISTILLERY FACTS

	Speyside		N/A
	1786		Feb.–mid-Mar. and
	Fons Bulliens' Well		Nov. Phone for
	2 wash 2 spirit		hours. Admission fee

TASTING NOTES

AGE: 12 years, 43%

NOSE: A beautiful aroma, full of summer fruit and flowers

TASTE: Light, sweet on the tongue, with hints of peat and caramel. Long, smooth, fruity finish.

"STRATHISLA"
PURE HIGHLAND MALT
SCOTCH WHISKY
THE OLDEST DISTILLERY IN THE HIGHLANDS
AGED 12 YEARS
70 cl   43% vol

TALISKER

TALISKER DISTILLERY, CARBOST, SKYE IV47 8SR
TEL: +44 (0) 1478 640203 FAX: +44 (0) 1478 640401

Talisker is the only distillery on the Isle of Skye and was built in 1830 by Hugh and Kenneth MacAskill. Talisker is situated in a sheltered glen on the west coast of the island, on the edge of the Loch Harport.

The story of Talisker is a checkered one and the distillery passed through many hands until it became part of the Distillers Co. Ltd. in 1925. Talisker is marketed by United Distillers as one of their Classic Malt range.

DISTILLERY FACTS

	Highland–Skye		N/A
	1830		Apr.–Oct.,
	Cnoc-nan-Speireag		Nov.–Mar. Phone
	2 wash 2 spirit		for times

TASTING NOTES

AGE: 10 years, 45.8%

NOSE: Full, sweet yet peaty

TASTE: A well-rounded, full-flavored malt with peat and honey and a lingering finish.

TAMDHU

TAMDHU DISTILLERY, KNOCKANDO, ABERLOUR **AB38 7RP**
TEL: **+44 (0) 1340 870221** FAX: **+44 (0) 1340 810255**

Tamdhu Distillery was built in 1896 by William Grant, a director of Highland Distilleries. It was a state-of-the-art distillery, and incorporated the latest devices, such as grain elevators and mechanical switchers for ease of production. It closed in 1928 until after World War II, and demand continued to grow until, in 1972, the number of stills was increased from two to four, and then two more were added in 1975.

DISTILLERY FACTS

	Speyside		3 wash 3 spirit
	1896		Mix of sherry and
	Private springs		refill casks
			No visitors

TASTING NOTES

AGE: Unaged, 40%

NOSE: A light, warm aroma with a hint of honey

TASTE: Medium flavor, fresh on the palate with overtones of apple and pear orchards, and a long, mellow finish.

TEANINCH

TEANINCH DISTILLERY, ALNESS, ROSS-SHIRE **IV17 0XB**
TEL: **+44 (0) 1349 882461** FAX: **+44 (0) 1349 883864**

Teaninch Distillery was built by Captain Hugh Munro in 1817. After initial difficulties in obtaining barley, production increased 30 times by the 1830s. In 1869 the lessee was John McGilchrist Ross, who gave up in 1895. The distillery was then taken over by Munro & Cameron of Elgin in 1898, and in 1904 Innes Cameron became the sole owner. Eventually, the distillery was acquired by Scottish Malt Distillers Ltd.

DISTILLERY FACTS

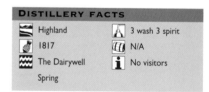

	Highland		3 wash 3 spirit
	1817		N/A
	The Dairywell		No visitors
	Spring		

TASTING NOTES

AGE: 23 years, distilled 1972, 64.95%

NOSE: Light, peaty

TASTE: Smoke and oak, with a long, mellow finish.

TOBERMORY

TOBERMORY DISTILLERY, TOBERMORY, ISLE OF MULL, ARGYLLSHIRE **PA75 6NR**
TEL: +44 (0) 1688 302645 FAX: +44 (0) 1688 302643

The distillery was founded in 1795 by John Sinclair, a local merchant. It became fully operational in 1823, but was silent between 1930 and 1972, when it was reopened as the Ledaig Distillery (Tobermory) Ltd. The company went into receivership in 1975 and was acquired by a Yorkshire property company. It closed again in 1989 and was purchased four years later by Burn Stewart Distillers.

DISTILLERY FACTS	
Highland–Mull	2 wash 2 spirit
1795	Refill
Private loch	Phone for times

TASTING NOTES

AGE: Tobermory unaged, 40%

NOSE: Light, soft, heathery

TASTE: Light, medium-flavored with undertones of honey and herbs, and a soft, smoky finish.

TOMATIN

TOMATIN DISTILLERY, TOMATIN, INVERNESS-SHIRE **IV13 7YT**
TEL +44 (0) 1808 511444 FAX: +44 (0) 1808 511373

Tomatin Distillery was founded in 1897. The company went into liquidation in 1906 and the distillery was reopened in 1909. In 1956 the number of stills was doubled to four and further were steadily added until, in 1974, there were 23. Tomatin eventually became a subsidiary of Takara Shuzo & Okura of Japan—the first distillery in Scotland to be purchased by a Japanese company.

DISTILLERY FACTS	
Highland	N/A
1897	Phone for times,
Allt na Frithe Burn	and group bookings
12 wash 11 spirit	

TASTING NOTES

AGE: 10 years, 40%

NOSE: A delicate aroma with hints of honey and smoke

TASTE: Light and smooth with a hint of peat.

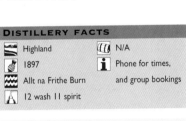

TOMINTOUL

TOMINTOUL, BALLINDALLOCH, BANFFSHIRE AB37 9AQ
TEL: +44 (0) 1807 590274 FAX: +44 (0) 1807 590342

Tomintoul is a modern distillery, built in 1964 and founded by a company called Hay & Macleod Ltd. along with W. & S. Strong Ltd., Glasgow whisky brokers. It was acquired by Scottish & Universal Investment Trust in 1973 and eventually became part of the Whyte & Mackay malt whisky portfolio. The number of stills was doubled to four in 1974. Tomintoul has a warm, coppery-gold color.

DISTILLERY FACTS

	Speyside		2 wash 2 spirit
	1964		N/A
	Ballantruan Spring		No visitors

TASTING NOTES

AGE: 10 years, 40%

NOSE: Light, sherry

TASTE: Sweet on the tongue with smoky undertones.

THE TORMORE

TORMORE DISTILLERY, ADVIE, GRANTOWN-ON-SPEY, MORAY PH26 3LR
TEL: +44 (0) 1807 510244 FAX: +44 (0) 1807 510352

This was the first new distillery to be built in the twentieth century in Scotland. The buildings and housing are built around a square with a belfry, which has a chiming clock. It was built for the Long John Group and eventually became part of the Allied Distillers portfolio. In 1972, the number of stills was increased from four to eight. Tormore is a golden malt with a well-rounded taste, recommended as an after-dinner drink.

DISTILLERY FACTS

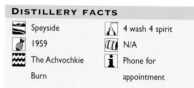

	Speyside		4 wash 4 spirit
	1959		N/A
	The Achvochkie Burn		Phone for appointment

TASTING NOTES

AGE: 10 years, 40%

NOSE: A dry aroma with a slightly nutty overtone

TASTE: Soft on the tongue; a well-defined, medium-flavored malt with a hint of honey.

YOICHI

HOKKAIDO DISTILLERY, KUROKAWA-CHO 7 CHOME-6, YOICHI-CHO, YOICHI-GUN, HOKKAIDO 046, JAPAN
TEL: +81 (0) 135 23 3131 FAX: +81 (0) 135 23 2202

When Masataka Taketsuru (see p. 67) returned from Scotland after studying whisky distilling at Glasgow University, he looked for a site with ideal conditions, and built a whisky distillery on Hokkaido Island at Yoichi. The site is surrounded by mountains on three sides, and the ocean on the fourth. Hokkaido is the northernmost Japanese island, with cool, clean air and a ready supply of water from underground springs rising through peat bogs.

This distinctive-looking distillery was built in 1934 and produces a vibrant copper-colored single malt whisky which is usually only available in Japan.

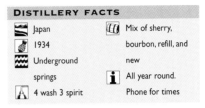

DISTILLERY FACTS

	Japan		Mix of sherry, bourbon, refill, and new
	1934		
	Underground springs		
	4 wash 3 spirit		All year round. Phone for times

TASTING NOTES

AGE: 12 years

NOSE: Peaty with a hint of sherry

TASTE: Full-bodied with a peaty taste and a long finish.

GLOSSARY OF TERMS

blended whisky Created from both single malts and grain whisky.

cask-strength whisky Whisky sold at the strength taken from the cask: normally 60% alcoholic volume or 120° proof.

Coffey stills Still invented by Aeneas Coffey in 1831. It allows for the continuous production of spirit without having to empty and refill pot stills.

cooper A craftsman skilled in making and repairing wooden barrels and casks.

Customs and Excise Officer's house Scottish Customs and Excise officers used to live on the site of a distillery, in a house provided by the distillery company, so that they could ensure that everything was carried out legally. This practice has now stopped.

draff The solids that remain at the base of the mash tun and are removed and used as cattle feed.

feints After the pure spirit has been taken off from the spirit still, the condensed vapor weakens and is no longer pure. This weakened spirit is known as feints and is discarded.

foreshots The first liquid produced in the spirit still, as the steam condenses. Foreshots turn cloudy when water is added as the spirit is still impure and is discarded.

grain whisky Produced using a continuous distillation process. Malted and unmalted cereals are used and the spirit is of a higher strength.

grist The dried malt is ground finely and is then known as grist.

lees The sediment of a liquor during fermentation and ageing.

lyne arms The top of a pot still bends to form an arm through which the spirit passes into the spirit still. The shape of these arms varies and distillery managers believe that the different arms contribute to the final characteristics of the whisky. One type is known as a lyne arm.

malted barley Germinated malt is known as malted barley when the enzymes in the barley have been released, giving barley its malty taste.

malting floor In a traditional distillery, barley is soaked in water for two or three days and then spread on a stone malting floor until germination takes place.

malt kiln A traditional method of drying malted barley is using smoke from a kiln usually burning peat. The smoke filters through a fine mesh to the barley above.

mashing Grist is then mixed with hot water in a mash tun.

mash tun Large circular vessel often made from copper, with a lid. Mechanical rakes move around inside the mash tun to ensure that the barley is mixed with the boiling water.

mothballed Some distilleries have been closed down for a while yet could reopen any time. The Scotch whisky industry talks of them as being mothballed. Everything is kept in pristine condition ready for reopening.

pot still A pot still produces whisky in batches and not continuously. See also Coffey still.

Saladin maltings A mechanically controlled method of germinating barley. The barley is placed in large rectangular boxes. Air is blown up through the grain at controlled temperatures and the grain is turned mechanically.

single cask whisky Whisky from just one cask or barrel, bottled usually in a numbered limited edition.

single malt whisky A whisky that is distilled at an individual distillery and produced only from malted barley. A bottle may include whisky from several years' production from the same distillery.

spent lees Waste material produced during distillation.

spirit stills These stills are used for the second distillation and spirit is collected from these to be stored in barrels.

stills These are traditionally made from copper and in the case of malt whisky distillation are also known as pot stills (q.v.).

triple distillation Triple-distilled single malt whisky is produced by passing the spirit through the spirit still twice.

vatted malt Produced by combining several malt whiskies from several distilleries.

wash The liquid drawn off from the mash tun is commonly called wort, but sometimes described as wash. See also wash stills.

wash stills The germinated liquid from the washbacks is pumped into these stills for the first distillation, which separates out the alcohol.

washbacks Large vessels, usually wooden, which can hold from 3,000 to 15,000 gallons. The liquid (known as wort) from the mash tun is pumped into the washbacks and yeast is added to convert the wort into alcohol.

whisky From the Celtic *usquebaugh* (Scots Gaelic *uisge beatha*, Irish Gaelic *uisce beathadh*, both adaptations of the Latin phrase *aqua vitae*, meaning "water of life").

wort The liquid drawn off from the mash tun is known as wort. The solid material resting at the bottom of the mash tun is used for cattle feed.

INDEX